the seeker's manual

ACHIEVE YOUR HIGHEST POTENTIAL
BY EXPLORING THE SYSTEM OF LIFE

arda

the seeker's manual

Library of Congress Catalog Number: 2013922005

ISBN 13 978-0-9898104-0-1

Printed in the United States of America

Cover Design by Elif Kuvvetli
Illustrations by Todd Harrison

for seekers everywhere

ACKNOWLEDGMENTS

WRITING THIS BOOK was an incredible journey. Even though it seems like a solitary activity, it's hardly a job of one person. I feel very lucky and blessed to have received help, guidance and support from so many people. Without them, this book wouldn't have come to fruition.

I'd like to express my deepest gratitude to:

My wife and soulmate, Elif, who has provided me so much unconditional love, friendship, understanding, inspiration, support and guidance, not only for the last two years on this project, but every day, since the first day we met twenty-three years ago.

My parents Samih and Guler and my sister Didem, who have always been there for me with their love, support and encouragement.

Naz McSweeney for opening the door to my personal and spiritual transformation. Her insightful guidance helped me understand the meaning of my life, recognize who I am and acquire a new perspective on life.

Master Zhao for introducing me to the world of life force energy. His teachings of Qigong meditation and energy healing techniques have transformed my life and given me the opportunity to work with energy. I'd like to also acknowledge that the techniques demonstrated in Illustrations 8, 9 and 10 are part of his teachings.

Sarah Perkins for her writing coaching and guidance on the content and the flow of the book, Lea Stublarec for her copy editing and creative ideas, Cindy Babyn for her edits and revisions, Sara Salem for proof reading, Daniel Rizk, Phillip Ziegler, Pavan Kochar, Julia Bernard, Mark Lennon, Anne Heffron, David Lisi, Rebecca Thomas, Rachel Grimes for their ideas, encouragements, support and insightful comments and Wendy Gayle for allowing me to use the becoming a tree breathing exercise shown in Illustration 14.

Last, but not least, my clients, whose trust in me and belief in the system of life made this manual a reality. Thank you!

CONTENTS

Letter to the Seeker

Dear Seeker,

Throughout my life, I have always been consciously aware of one particular burning question, "Am I ever going to make it in life?"

I grew up in Turkey, mostly in Istanbul. I remember this worrisome question weighing heavily on my mind since the first grade. The pressure wasn't just coming from my parents. It was from everyone—my teachers, community and society. Everybody expected me to be successful. So I studied hard and got into one of the best high schools, then into one of the best colleges, then into the best possible career that ensured financial security, then into the best company that provided the best future.

Buried under this pressure, I couldn't and didn't leave anything to chance. I felt I had to work relentlessly to secure a bright and successful future. Every little moment, every little decision carried so much importance about my future. I felt that one bad choice could ruin my entire life. Stakes were high. Pressure was enormous. Life was overwhelming. I felt powerless—it felt like I had to win against life. I had to make it in life.

After graduating from college, I immediately joined one of the Big 4 public accounting firms in Istanbul. Two years later, I left the firm to move to Sydney, Australia. While living in Sydney, I was surprised to find out that whomever I met expressed the same worries that I had about life. It was an astounding realization to me. I always thought that the pressure to make it and the sense of powerlessness came from growing up in a developing country. I felt that working hard and securing one's future was more crucial to one's survival there because the resources were limited.

I lived in Sydney for five years and got a transfer to another Big 4 public accounting firm in Silicon Valley, California. After I moved to the San Francisco Bay Area, I observed similar worries in others. Feeling powerless against life was universal. It was puzzling to me that no matter how many resources we had, how much success we achieved, how loving our relationships were, we all worried about future.

One of the reasons for our worry is that we feel unsafe. Life seems unpredictable and therefore imposes a major risk to our sense of security. Due to our survival instinct, we become naturally individualistic, trying to secure our own future. We accumulate material possessions or have sensory experiences in our attempts to feel safe. We sometimes get a glimpse of power that makes us feel safer, which, unfortunately, seems to fade away quickly. Failing to hold on to that moment of power, hence the security, we feel even more powerless.

Is life really that unreliable and overwhelming that we should live in constant fear and worry? Or is there a reason or meaning to what we experience?

As you hold *The Seeker's Manual* in your hands, I hope you join me in attempting to answer these questions. Let's explore together the meaning of life and the intricacies of how life flows. At heart, we are all seekers. And as seekers, we owe it to ourselves to explore life to find answers to our questions and achieve our highest potential.

The opportunity for my exploration came in July 2006, when I fell victim to stress and anxiety. My health, through chronic headaches and monthly episodes of sinus infections and bronchitis, was deteriorating quickly. I was constantly sick. I felt exhausted and depleted—physically and emotionally. Everything within me and around me seemed dark.

The attempts to get out of this darkness became the first steps of a journey that would provide me with a lot of answers about the meaning of life and how life flows. Everything started with trying to find a treatment for my stress and anxiety. As a fairly successful and ambitious finance executive at the time, all I wanted to do was to feel better so that I could be more productive at work and active in my life. When I looked at possible treatments, I realized that I didn't want to just address the symptoms. I wanted to get to the bottom of my health issues. So even though I was a skeptic at first, I turned to alternative healing practitioners and meditation teachers for solutions.

I knew meditation was a great tool that could help me cope with stress and anxiety, but it was still a big challenge to meditate in the beginning. I couldn't allocate time to meditate in my busy schedule. On rare occasions, when I found the time, I would realize that my mind would be so active that I couldn't sit still for more than two minutes. After many attempts and setbacks over a period of six months, to my surprise, I was able to establish a somewhat regular three-minute meditation practice. Soon thereafter, I realized something shocking. I noticed that, on the days I meditated, I felt substantially better and the flow of my life improved tremendously. This improvement was very encouraging. I couldn't afford not to continue to meditate. So I allocated more time to my meditation practice.

The tight correlation between the regularity of my meditation practice and the noticeable improvement in the flow of my life was really astonishing. I didn't get it. How could this correlation even be possible? I wanted to explore this phenomenon more. I started researching different philosophies and teachings. While applying some of the principles of these different modalities, I started to gain a fresh perspective on my own life.

As I acquired more self-knowledge and deeper understanding of my life, I discovered yet another tight correlation. This time, it was between my self-awareness and my life flow. Whenever I acquired a deeper self-knowledge and gained a new insight into an area of my life, I noticed a positive shift in the flow of my life. The shift was subtle, but impactful—and definitely very interesting. Soon I realized I was catching glimpses of a logical and meaningful order to life.

As part of this new shift in my life flow, new opportunities began to emerge. Whether it was someone I met, a seminar I attended, or a book I read, these new opportunities expanded my horizon. Whenever I welcomed a particular opportunity, my life seemed to open up to other possibilities. As life flowed better, more opportunities started appearing in front of me. It was very interesting how things seemed to magically come to me, without visualizing, intending or planning. All I did was embrace the opportunity that seemed most appealing and aligned with my values; nothing else.

I treated these opportunities like doors. This concept of "doors" made me realize I was the one holding the key to these opportunities. In other words, it was *I* who needed to take actions and open the doors to move forward—out of darkness toward healing. As I continued walking through the doors, one after the other, my health and the flow of my life kept improving. Note that I was still a skeptic. But, being skeptical didn't keep me from observing my experiences with an open mind and objectively acknowledging the positive shift in my life.

For example, while exploring ways to manage my stress and anxiety, one day I found myself attending a Reiki workshop, a Japanese energy healing modality. This was a completely new experience for me. Then, my Qigong meditation teacher invited me to participate in Qigong Energy Healing workshop. While learning these different modalities, a friend of mine suggested that I attend a Hypnotherapy certification program, and then another friend invited me to an Emotional Freedom Technique workshop. I didn't know at the time that I would incorporate some of these techniques into my healing practice one day. Looking back, it seems like I have intuitively followed a magical path.

I didn't know where this path was leading, nor did I have any specific plans or expectations about where it should take me. When I walked through one door, another opportunity would arrive. Interesting synchronicities started to happen. It was amazing that as soon as I learned a new technique, I would get a chance to practice it on someone, be it a family member or a friend or a colleague. Our conversation would almost always lead us to the stress they experience in their lives. After learning about what

I had gone through they would be curious and allow me to do some energy work on their headache, shoulder pain or stiff neck. Other times, it would be their emotional discomfort I would help them with.

The fascinating part was that I was simply walking on a path, without any intention of quitting my job or becoming a wellness coach or opening an energy healing practice one day. Even though I didn't have any specific goals in mind, the process didn't feel random. The path that I was on was not a coincidence. For the first time in my life, I was on a beautiful flow. I felt that life was on my side. I was excited and energized about my life. I felt a deeper connection to my family and friends. I started forming compassionate relationships with everybody around me. The energy work I started to do gave me fulfillment, as I was able to discover my unique skill set and help others. I felt that I was walking towards my highest potential. For me, there was no turning back.

I left my 20-year finance career in February 2011 to start my coaching and healing practice. It was very clear to me that I was answering my calling. Life simply showed me the way by bringing series of opportunities in front of me. Was everything a coincidence or someone else could experience a similar magical flow and follow their own path to achieve their highest potential?

To me, this was the ultimate question that would prove whether or not a logical system existed in life. Time and time again, I have seen my clients live through similar experiences and go through the same steps that ultimately help them transform their lives, enhance their well-being and achieve their highest potential. The answer was in front of me. These transformative experiences my clients had proved to me that, beyond any doubt, an identifiable system exists in life and exploring such system leads everyone to their highest potential.

Walking on a path of personal transformation is a journey—and let me tell you that such a journey doesn't necessarily mean quitting your job or ending your relationships or experiencing a fundamental change in your life. The journey simply helps you answer questions such as: *Who am I? What is the meaning of my life? How can I connect with my calling and find my life's work? How can I form loving and compassionate relationships? How can I live a joyful and fulfilling life and achieve my highest potential?*

The Seeker's Manual will help you gain deeper insights into these questions. You will learn about the meaning of your life and get to know who you are. With every little bit of self-knowledge, you will feel like you are getting closer to your calling and to your highest potential. What your highest potential will look like is up to you, and what you do with it depends solely on you.

A journey of this magnitude is not easy. Having been on this journey for a while and guiding my clients through similar experiences in their own transformation journeys, I felt that I was able to identify a logical and energy-based approach that anyone can use for their own transformation.

My hope is that *The Seeker's Manual* provides the blueprint for your personal transformation journey so that you can understand your experience more fully and deeply, as well as know exactly where you are on your journey.

The step-by-step guidance and practices provided in this manual will alleviate the difficulties and challenges that one expects to face in a transformation journey. Through exploring the system of life, you will know exactly what actions to take and what blockages to remove in order to connect with your unique path towards achieving your highest potential.

Let's not waste any more time! Let's explore the meaning of life together. As someone who has been walking on his path for a while and who is still on his journey seeking deeper fulfillment and inner calmness, I share your excitement and understand your fear of the unknown. I congratulate you on taking this important step towards enhancing your life, and I honor your courage in choosing to discover your highest potential.

With love and light,
arda
Palo Alto, California
January 2014

1 · Underlying Principles

THE SEEKER'S MANUAL lays out the blueprint of a personal transformation journey for self-realization. It describes in detail the
specific steps that you need to take to achieve your highest potential. Before we dive into the details of this journey, I'd like to
first go through the following underlying principles that are the
building blocks of the concepts explored in *The Seeker's Manual*.

Experiencing Life as Energy

We are all energy beings. Our physical bodies are composed of
atoms, which are a form of energy. We also have an energy body
that surrounds and permeates us. This energy body is something
we feel if we are tuned in, though most of us can't see it. Knowing that we are energy beings has two important implications on
the transformation journey.

The first implication of being energy is that we record all of
our life experiences within our energy body. Imagine this subtle
energy body as a database where we store our thoughts and emotions. The important thing to note here is that we record an experience according to what it means to us, in other words, how we
interpret it. We wire our experiences and related interpretations

into our energy body. We unconsciously access this information when a similar situation arises. Due to our energetic wiring, accessing the appropriate data is automatic and immediate. Using this information, we interpret future life situations and act accordingly.

Secondly, as energy beings, we possess gravitational power. What does this mean? It means that we have the ability to pull situations and people into our lives. Our experience today is what we have attracted to our life according to our energy level. We don't exactly know what we will experience in life, but we have control over our energy level. Through this control, we can directly influence the quality of our experiences. Our energy level begets our experience.

In this manual, I will explain how to raise our energy level so that we can attract better life experiences and achieve our highest potential. In order to learn how to manage our energy level, we need to shift our mindset and focus on our own life. If we want a better future, we have to look at what we have attracted today. This approach represents a major change in our perspective on how we experience life. By only utilizing our current life experiences, we can take appropriate actions to raise our energy level and, as a result, shift the current flow of our life for the better.

Let's review a specific life situation. Suppose that growing up, your parents compared your school performance to your friends or criticized you constantly for not being a good, smart or talented kid or perhaps you compared yourself to your high achieving older siblings. Every time you experienced one of these situations, you interpreted it as though your parents and others thought that you were not good enough.

One experience after the other, you energetically wire the thought and the belief within your energy body that your parents, siblings, friends and everybody else, including you, think that you are not good enough. In every occasion thereafter, you access this thought pattern and belief system and interpret your parents' comparison to your friends or your siblings' achievements as a sign that you are not good enough. As an energy being, you start to attract specific situations and people that constantly trigger your thought patterns and belief systems.

Life Conditioning—Birth of Initial Persona

Life conditioning is the way our life experiences influence our thought patterns and belief systems. When we identify ourselves with our life conditioning, the thoughts and beliefs become in-grained within our mind and form our first identity—our initial persona.

As a child, growing up, we may interpret many experiences as traumatic. Under our survival mode, we want to protect ourselves and therefore, subconsciously, let the lessons learned from these traumatic events form our thought patterns and belief systems. Note that a traumatic event to a child may not be an obvious one. For example, if our parents were late to pick us up from school a few times, we might have felt worthless, abandoned and therefore, not loved. We might assume that we were not worth their love and care, and form our thoughts and beliefs accordingly.

Over time, these thought patterns and belief systems influence our perceptions and give meaning to what we experience. For example, when we think and believe that we are not worth for our parents' love and care, we keep looking at their actions from that perspective. Do they love us? Do they care for us? With every little disappointment and unmet expectation, we conclude again that we are worthless and our parents don't love us and care for us.

Once we start to view our life situations through the lens of our perceptions—based on our life conditioning, we see everything in one color. We categorize situations according to what we think and believe they are and how we think they relate to us. We then respond to life according to these interpretations and live a distorted reality we created in our mind.

Eventually, our life conditioning becomes our programming. Like a well-programmed robot, we assume our identity in this distorted reality and adopt our initial thought patterns and belief systems. These may be that we are worthless, not good enough, not lovable, not successful, not good looking or not smart—whatever our life conditioning is, we feel it's real. Our initial programming becomes our reality. We slowly start to identify ourselves with whom we think and believe we are and how we perceive the world sees us. Our initial persona is born.

Continuing with the previous hypothetical situation, where you interpreted your parents' comparison and criticism as not being good enough for them. You thought and believed that if you were better, your parents would love you. However, what your parents really wanted to do was for you to do better and be more successful, so that you are happy and prosper in life. To that extent, they just wanted to motivate you by giving you examples of how other kids do better at school or help you learn from your mistakes by correcting your actions. They didn't know any other way to clearly communicate their message to you. They did what they could. However, you interpreted their words and comments as comparisons or criticisms. You believed they thought you were not good enough. These interpretations formed your thought patterns and belief systems. They got wired within your energy body as your life conditioning and became part of your initial persona.

Feeling Vulnerable and Underlying Fears

Our initial thoughts and beliefs are not unfounded. Even though they seem to be harsh and self-bashing, they are absolutely reasonable and justifiable according to the way we interpret our experiences. Our initial persona assumes these unpleasant thoughts and beliefs as real and starts to feel vulnerable. We start to worry about how we will make it in this world if we are indeed not good enough, not lovable, not successful, not good looking or not smart. Every thought pattern and belief system that created the initial persona turns into an underlying fear.

A major issue then becomes how we can feel so vulnerable, yet find the strength to move forward. When our vulnerability creates a fear based living, our survival instinct provides our strength. Like all other living beings, feeling safe and fighting for our safety is our primal instinct. Due to this survival mode, we quickly learn how to protect ourselves at all costs. We don't want people to see our vulnerability. We can't afford to show anybody our initial persona—how vulnerable we feel inside. We don't want anybody to know who we really think and believe we are. In order to feel safe and fit in, we need to hide our vulnerability and disguise our initial persona.

Your initial thought patterns and belief systems of not being good enough are now your underlying fears: "Oh no! I must not be good enough. But, how am I going to make it in life?" As part of your initial persona, you carry these thoughts and beliefs and now underlying fears along with you wherever you go. Affected by your life conditioning, you perceive situations and people as a threat to your survival. You become sensitive and take things personally when your boss criticizes your work or when your spouse compares you to your friend or you see someone else succeed or receive recognition. You perceive that people think you are not good enough and want to get away from them and hide your vulnerability.

Conditioned Self—The Antagonist

The conditioned self is the identity we develop to hide our vulnerability and disguise our initial persona. Our conditioned self is the product of our survival instinct. We reject our vulnerability and refuse to live as our initial persona, so we create the antagonist, our conditioned self.

The development of our conditioned self is a gradual process. As we grow up and form our initial thought patterns and belief systems, we want to feel loved and accepted so that we can cope with our vulnerability and underlying fears. Therefore, we quickly begin to learn new behaviors and adopt new actions to conform to others' rules about what to do or how to think. On other occasions, our parents, mentors or teachers label us as whom we shall become. We may decide to assume the suggested identity and work towards it. We slowly start molding ourselves into this conditioned self who appropriately responds to others' expectations and finds ways to fit in and comply with their rules.

Not all of us choose to conform to others' rules. Some of us completely go against others' expectations, and take a different set of actions to do just the opposite of what is expected. In these situations, in order to fit in and feel safe, we may connect with others who have made similar rebellious choices. Of course, each of us is a unique individual. There are different possibilities among the conforming and non-conforming courses of action that we choose in order to develop our conditioned self.

Either way, no matter what choices we make, we develop our conditioned self to hide our initial persona and disguise our initial life conditioning so that we feel safer. We form our own conditioned thought patterns and belief systems to cope with our vulnerability and fight off our underlying fears. We push our initial persona deep down inside ourselves. This new conditioned self becomes our mask to the outside world. We identify ourselves with this mask and others recognize us by that identity.

For example, if you think and believe deep down that you are not good enough, then you may have conditioned yourself to be someone who is a perfectionist, or a hard worker who wants to be recognized for accomplishments, or an overly cautious person who has an eye for detail to avoid making mistakes, all so that you can cover your initial persona's vulnerability and underlying fear that you are not good enough.

In another possible example, if you think and believe deep down that you are not lovable, then you may have conditioned yourself to please others, or say yes to things that you don't want to do, or go out of your way to accommodate others, all so that you can receive love and appreciation.

7

Repressed Thoughts and Emotions

Repressed thoughts and emotions are the cognitions and feelings that we withhold, suppress and ignore during a traumatic event.

While developing our conditioned self, we create the formula of how to survive in this world. Even though we manage to hide our vulnerability and disguise our initial persona behind the mask of our conditioned self, we avoid addressing our underlying fears. Not having dealt with our vulnerability directly, we become anxious and fearful that somehow our initial persona will be exposed.

Keeping our underlying fears deep inside makes us feel more vulnerable to the outside world. Even though we operate under the disguise of our conditioned self so that we feel safe, we are still aware of our vulnerability. In order to keep up with the appearances of our conditioned self, we withdraw into our comfort zone and avoid fully expressing what is in our mind and heart. If we did express what we really thought or felt, we would expose our vulnerability.

As a result, repressing our thoughts and emotions becomes second nature to us. Whenever we are exposed to a situation or person that triggers these feelings, we immediately show an intense emotional reaction to defend our vulnerability. We take it personally because we perceive it as an attack to our conditioned self. We try to ward off the threat by immediately launching our defense mechanisms, such as getting angry with people or blaming circumstances or avoiding certain situations. While defending our conditioned self, we repress our *true* thoughts and emotions even more, so that we can effectively hide our vulnerability.

Suppose your boss criticized your work and told you that

the quality of your work was disappointing. In another scenario, imagine that your spouse compared you unfavorably to your friend. On another occasion, say that you saw someone receive an award at work or get promoted to a position that you felt you deserved. What would you do when all these situations stir up your initial thought pattern and belief system of not being good enough?

Your reaction may be to get angry with your boss or get frustrated with your spouse or be jealous that someone else has gotten the recognition. Right after you feel these intense emotional reactions, you may immediately start launching your defense mechanisms. You may vent to your friends about the unfairness of your boss. You may get into an argument with your spouse or choose not talk to them for a while. Still upset, you may walk around with a long face, indulge yourself with overeating, watch too much TV, or drink excessively.

While using these defense mechanisms to protect your conditioned self against any challenging and difficult situations, you don't directly address your true thoughts and emotions. You just apply your defense mechanisms, so that you can cover up your vulnerability and move on. If you decide to review your specific defense mechanisms, you will notice that you have conditioned your responses to specific situations and people. Your defense mechanisms will be very similar in how you respond to your boss' criticism, your spouse's comparison or your colleague's promotion. Instead of facing your vulnerability and getting in touch with your initial thought patterns and belief systems, you have created these similar strategies to defend your conditioned self and hide your vulnerability.

Consequently, the thought and the feeling of not being good enough remain repressed within your energy body.

Energy Blockages

Energy blockages are the bubbles that store our thoughts and emotions that we repress during a traumatic event.

We form our initial thought patterns and belief systems during traumatic events that make us feel vulnerable. Because we feel extremely fearful at that time, we get defensive. Even though we react with the most intense emotions to defend ourselves, we bury the emotionally painful experience into our energy body. These repressed thoughts and emotions become our energy blockages.

Energy blockages are part of life. We all have them. We need to learn about them as they carry clues about our initial thought patterns and belief systems and related underlying fears. Without addressing why and how we have formed our energy blockages in the first place, we will not be able to understand our life conditioning and eliminate emotional pain and suffering in our life. By getting in touch with our past, we can access our initial persona and our repressed thoughts and emotions. Through this deeper understanding, we can work on overcoming our underlying fears and releasing related energy blockages. Only then can we completely free ourselves from the layers of our life conditioning, liberate our initial persona, unmask our conditioned self and find our way towards our highest potential.

Now, think about your childhood. Even if you had connected with your true thoughts and feelings of being not good enough, do you think that you would have felt the courage to tell your parents at the time of a traumatic situation how they made you feel? How could you? Even today, as your conditioned self, you keep repressing most of your true thoughts and emotions. Instead of expressing yourself fully, you immediately launch your defense mechanisms and try to ward off a perceived attack coming from your spouse, family, colleagues or friends.

Nobody is at fault here. In most of the situations, without self-awareness, you may not have access to what you truly think and feel. You have repressed them for so long. Back then, during a traumatic event, you may have completely blocked your true thoughts and emotions. Nonetheless, you felt the emotional pain when your parents made you feel not good enough. Their actions and words have made you feel vulnerable and you then repressed your thoughts and emotions. Your energy blockages started to form from these early incidents.

Limiting Life Patterns

Limiting life patterns are the situations and people who repeatedly come into our lives and poke at our vulnerability.

Here comes the beauty of life. We don't need to remember what incident it was exactly that formed our initial thought patterns and belief systems, and related energy blockages. All we need to do is to look at our life today. Everything we need to know is right here, in front of us.

As mentioned earlier, one of the implications of being energy is that we attract situations and people into our lives. Our energy blockages determine the specifics of what we attract. As a result, we keep experiencing the seemingly unrelated events that constantly poke at our vulnerability and provoke our underlying fears. Without addressing our energy blockages and what's captured within them, we keep experiencing our limiting life patterns, and feel stuck in them.

In order to break these limiting patterns, we need to start utilizing the information available in them. In reality, they provide us with an opportunity to learn about our vulnerability and underlying fears, so that we get to know our conditioned self and initial persona and understand our life conditioning. All we need to do is to identify and acknowledge those situations and people that repeatedly poke at our underlying fears. Only through that acknowledgement can we dig deeply into our initial thought patterns and belief systems that created our vulnerability. Once we understand our underlying fears and recognize our vulnerability, we will be able to release our energy blockages. Without energy blockages that attract the events provoking our underlying fears, our limiting life patterns will subside.

Here are some examples of common life patterns that most of us face on a regular basis:

- *dating the same type of person over and over again*

- *getting constantly frustrated by the same words, comments or actions from a loved one*

- *getting sick before or after an important event*

- *reporting to the same type of boss wherever we work*

- *procrastinating before an important deadline or major project*

- *getting into the same arguments and having the same conflicts over and over again*

Now take a moment and observe your life. Do you notice any particular life pattern that you consistently experience? While contemplating your own life patterns, let's apply this new information to our hypothetical example that you have an energy blockage related to the repressed thought and emotion of being not good enough. When you interact with your boss, with your spouse or with your parents—yes even today—do they trigger the feeling of being not good enough? Can you think about a time when this kind of trigger occurred?

Energy Level

Energy level is the frequency that our energy vibrates at.

Let's explore further what really goes on in terms of our limiting life patterns and what we pull or attract into our lives. Since we are energy beings, we vibrate at a certain frequency. This frequency determines our energy level. Our energy level is an important measurement because there is a direct correlation between our energy level and the quality of our experiences. The lower our energy level is, the more challenging situations and the more difficult people we encounter—and the higher it is, the lesser the situations and people will poke at our underlying fears and threaten our vulnerability.

How can we then determine where our energy level is? We can't and we don't need to. All we need to know is that energy blockages bring our energy level down. All negative thoughts and emotions have low vibration. Because energy blockages contain the negative thoughts and emotions that are repressed during a moment of vulnerability, they naturally lower our overall energy level.

In order to recognize the specific impact that our energy blockages have on our energy level and, hence, on the quality of our life, we need to look at what we are experiencing today. We can easily understand where our energy level is by observing our current life flow. Through such observation, we can see what we have already attracted, learn about the life pattern we are in, and understand exactly what underlying fears a particular situation or person triggers. Since our energy blockages attract such events, we will be able to take actions to directly address our repressed thoughts and emotions, release related energy blockages and raise our energy level.

As we start vibrating at a higher frequency, our limiting life patterns lose their intensity. We start to attract better opportunities that are aligned with our higher energy level and bring us closer to our highest potential.

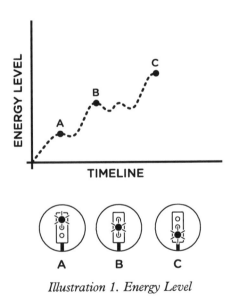

Illustration 1. Energy Level

The correlation between our energy level and the quality of our life flow is astounding. When our energy level is low, we are constantly getting red lights. In other words, we regularly experience roadblocks, difficulties, setbacks, and adversity in our life flow. When our energy level is higher, our life flow will start to shift. The lights will turn to yellow first. Then, as our vibration increases, the lights will turn to green and we will have longer periods of a beautiful, uninterrupted, comfortable and fulfilling ride.

So why are we stuck at these low energy levels and keep running into red lights? Instead of addressing our energy blockages directly, we keep launching our defense mechanisms to ward off attacks to our conditioned self. We just use them to hide our vulnerability. As a result, our true thoughts and emotions remain repressed, lowering our vibration and keeping us stuck at red light.

In addition, our defense mechanisms require effort. We spend a lot of energy when we defend our conditioned self. Thus, we remain within the same energy level, attracting the same life situations and people. In order to attract a better life flow, we need to take different actions that will raise our energy level and change the quality of our life.

Taking such actions requires courage and inner power. Through the study of *The Seeker's Manual*, you will be able to access these key energies that will empower you and enable you to break your limiting life patterns, so that you can attract a better life flow and make progress towards achieving your highest potential.

Let's review a few examples of such actions that will change your energy level. For example, next time, when you get angry with someone who makes you feel not good enough, instead of getting defensive, can you stand up and tell them how their comments affected you? In those situations, can you recognize your underlying fears and admit your vulnerability of feeling not good enough, even to yourself? Whenever you feel vulnerable and want to withdraw from everything, will you be able to do something different in your life that comes from your heart that will nurture your mind, body and soul and bring joy into your life?

Note that we have been using "not good enough" as a general example because it's a common vulnerability most of us have. At this point, you might be aware of your own specific vulnerability. If so, replace not good enough with your own initial thought patterns and belief systems such as being unlovable, unworthy, not recognized, not successful or any other thought or belief that your own initial persona may have.

Highest Potential

Highest potential is the maximum energy level we can reach where the flow of life is joyful and fulfilling.

Specifically, highest potential means having a constant presence of a mentally and physically healthy body that radiates energy and well-being. It means having loving and compassionate relationships with everyone in our life. It means having satisfying and fulfilling work that utilizes our unique skill set and creativity. It means having a deeper connection with our environment and world around us. It also means reaching an inner calmness and having the peace of mind that comes from getting to know who we are and understanding the meaning of our life.

As suggested in the previous example, once you start taking

actions to specifically address your "not good enough" energy blockage, you will notice a shift in your energy level. Courage and inner power that you gain through your actions will raise the frequency of your vibration. At these new heights of your energy level, you will start to realize that your limiting life patterns begin to disintegrate. Instead of draining your energy to hide your vulnerability and fight against your life patterns, you will start to preserve your energy for nurturing your body, mind and spirit, forming loving and compassionate relationships, utilizing your unique skill set, living joyfully and expressing your authenticity. Having limiting life patterns out of your way, you now have your eyes set on achieving your highest potential.

System of Life

Before you begin to take the steps described in *The Seeker's Manual* towards your highest potential, let's spend a brief moment reviewing how the underlying principles fit together as the system of life:

Since the day we were born, we have been exposed to traumatic events as part of our life experiences. Even though, growing up, we may have experienced happy and beautiful moments, we have also been exposed to circumstances that make us feel unsafe, uncomfortable, uneasy and unhappy. Due to their emotional impact, these life experiences shape our initial persona. We feel even more vulnerable and powerless when we realize later on that our efforts to run away from these emotionally painful circumstances are in vain. No matter how much we try to avoid them, we keep running into similar situations throughout our lives.

Running into what we want to escape from is not a coincidence; it's the system of life.

Here is how it works.

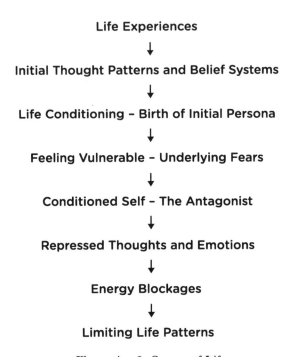

Life Experiences

↓

Initial Thought Patterns and Belief Systems

↓

Life Conditioning – Birth of Initial Persona

↓

Feeling Vulnerable – Underlying Fears

↓

Conditioned Self – The Antagonist

↓

Repressed Thoughts and Emotions

↓

Energy Blockages

↓

Limiting Life Patterns

Illustration 2. System of Life

The initial traumatic events that we experience create our initial thought patterns and belief systems and become our life conditioning. When we identify ourselves with our life conditioning, we integrate these thoughts and beliefs into our identity and form our initial persona. We bury the experience of the traumatic event within our energy body, into our energy blockages, and cover the underlying fears of our initial persona along with our repressed thoughts and emotions. Feeling fearful and unsafe, we create a mask to hide our vulnerability. We develop our conditioned self. We program ourselves *to be* our conditioned self. Like a software program, we start to operate under our source code—someone presses a button, and we display exactly what we are supposed to—the way we have programmed ourselves. We become very rigid and predictable. We feel vulnerable and take it personally whenever someone challenges the identity of our conditioned self. We know exactly what to do, how to react, what to feel. We learn the most effective ways to defend our conditioned self. We get robotic. As a result, we keep reacting to life situations in a predictable manner. The same type of people keeps annoying us. We go through the same routine over and over again without realizing the thought patterns and belief systems of our initial persona that make us feel vulnerable and ignite our defensive actions.

As part of the system of life, our energy blockages keep attracting situations and people into our lives that poke at our specific underlying fears and make us feel vulnerable. Under the mask of our conditioned self, in order to avoid exposing our vulnerability, we repress our thoughts and emotions even further—instead of directly dealing with them. Without gaining a deeper understanding of our energy blockages and related underlying fears, we keep trying to defend our conditioned self and stay exposed to our limiting life patterns.

These life patterns are not pleasant and may prove to be challenging and difficult at times. We feel powerless because we don't know how to get out of them. We feel trapped, as they constantly repeat in our lives. We feel life is chaotic, complex and overwhelming. We sometimes lose hope and feel that these limiting life patterns are here to stay and will torment us forever.

In these times, life seems to be working against us.

By changing our perspective, we can understand that our life patterns are there for a reason. Fortunately and paradoxically, even though we may feel that these challenging life patterns are like our biggest roadblocks in achieving our highest potential, they actually provide us with the self-knowledge that's necessary to progress on our journey.

When we review the system of life, one important message stands out very clearly:

The purpose of life is to get to know our conditioned self and initial persona and understand our life conditioning. Only then can we release our energy blockages and break our limiting life patterns to answer our calling. By responding to our calling, we can find our unique place in the world and understand the meaning of our life. With that deep insight, we can attain joy, gratitude, fulfillment and inner calmness and deeply connect with one another in loving and compassionate relationships.

The system of life is beautiful, ingenious and divine. It provides us with the challenging and limiting life patterns that show us the meaning of our life and who we are. Once we open ourselves up to the opportunities in front of us and become courageous and powerful enough to take the necessary actions to face our underlying fears, release our energy blockages and raise our energy level, the system of life simply guides us along the path that leads to our highest potential. Let's explore this system together. Let's learn about the meaning of our life. Let's find out who we really are. Let's take some conscious actions to raise our energy level and break our limiting life patterns. It's time to take ownership of our lives and achieve our highest potential.

2 • The Journey Within

WE ALL ARE in a constant search for happiness. As long as we look outside of ourselves for happiness, this search is pointless. It is merely an unsuccessful attempt to escape from what we don't want to face in our current life. In reality, the escape is from our initial persona and our underlying fears. Under the influence of our innate survival instinct, we equate happiness to feeling safe and define happiness as being loved, connected, respected, liked, included, recognized, and successful. We program our conditioned self to acquire and accumulate things, and to have the right sensory experiences, so that we find happiness and feel safe.

Searching for happiness is fine. Sometimes you get what you look for. You think by achieving whatever you have worked hard for will make you happy. What happens then? Over time you don't feel fulfilled enough. You feel that something is still missing. Since you haven't directly addressed your underlying fears, your vulnerability is intact. You still feel powerless. Your initial persona still feels vulnerable. You feel that you are back in survival mode again. Realizing nothing has changed, you immediately start chasing something else to be happy. You stay in this vicious cycle throughout your life. The constant chase and search for happiness takes a lot of effort and brings your energy level down. When your energy level is low, you feel more vulnerable and less safe.

This energy drainage depletes your body, mind and spirit. Instead of looking outside for happiness, how about redirecting your focus inward, where you can find traces of your life conditioning that is limiting your life? Only by learning about your initial persona and your vulnerability can you conquer your underlying fears, release the energy blockages, free yourself from emotional pain and suffering and live a joyful and fulfilling life. This inward focus is your journey within.

Phases of the Journey Within

The journey within is one of self-realization where you transform your initial persona and conditioned self, who are buried under the layers of your life conditioning to your authentic self—your true essence waiting to emerge.

Even though every one of us is unique and has had different life experiences, our individual journeys have the same identifiable phases. By taking the actions required for each phase, you will soon start to peel off the layers of your life conditioning and liberate your initial persona from your underlying fears so that you can unmask your conditioned self and finally meet your authentic self and achieve your highest potential.

Any journey of such magnitude is not easy. It is a life-long process. You don't need to know from the start of your journey who your authentic self is or what you are supposed to do with your life. You don't need to connect with your calling, or know your life's work, right away. Such connection will take time. But, don't worry, while following the guidance in this manual, you will slowly find your calling. You will experience how your authentic self will naturally emerge. In the beginning, all you need to do is to take actions to break your limiting life patterns. Your energy level will then naturally increase and connect you with the best life flow that is aligned with your essence.

In order to raise your energy level, *The Seeker's Manual* offers specific key practices that are relevant to each phase. Each key practice will help you access and open up a particular key energy within your body for the relevant phase. This key energy is a sensation, a state of mind or an inner feeling that you will connect to when you apply the specific principles of each phase and master the key practice. Thus, you will not only study the concepts of your journey, but also feel these concepts energetically in your body.

The recommended key practices included in *The Seeker's Manual* are the ones I have found useful and effective on my journey. They have helped me break my limiting life patterns. I also had a chance to observe their impact on my clients. In terms of number of spiritual practices and alternative tools that are available to us, we live in abundant times. There are so many different methods, meditation techniques, prayers, visualizations and rituals, all of which have been proven to help and guide many people. Therefore, if you have other effective and empowering practices that provide you with the key energies you need for your particular challenging life situations, please continue practicing them. Whatever you do, though, diligently incorporate them into your daily routine. Allocate enough time to practice them. Observe their effectiveness and how empowering they are in your life.

The Seven-Phase Journey

A typical transformation journey consists of seven phases. Each one of these phases emphasizes the necessary steps and strategies to reach the relevant energy levels necessary for completing your journey. Along with the specific actions you need to take, each phase provides you with the opportunity to gain a new perspective on your life.

Keep in mind that completing one phase doesn't necessarily mean that you are done with that phase. Later on, you may need to return to some phases to strengthen the key energies that you need for the rest of your journey. As you progress further, you will realize that the phases follow an order. In order to connect with the energy of one phase, you need to have accessed the key energies of previous phases.

Knowing the phases helps you figure out where you are on your journey. Each phase is a building block of your new life of higher energy levels. Approach your journey with a sense of deep curiosity and enthusiasm. You will be meeting your authentic self soon. What journey could be more joyful and rewarding than this one?!

Here are the seven phases of your journey within:

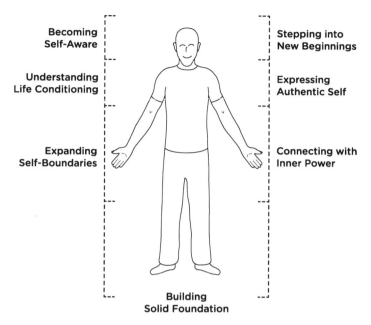

Becoming
Self-Aware

Understanding
Life Conditioning

Expanding
Self-Boundaries

Stepping into
New Beginnings

Expressing
Authentic Self

Connecting with
Inner Power

Building
Solid Foundation

Illustration 3. Phases of the Journey

Phase 1: Becoming Self-Aware

The first phase of your journey is about getting to know your conditioned self and becoming aware of your initial persona and your life conditioning.

During this phase, you will learn how to identify your limiting life patterns so that you can start observing the actions of your conditioned self in them. Your self-awareness process starts with recognizing your intense emotional reactions, as your emotions are the best guides to help you identify your trigger events and discover your perceptions.

You naturally show intense emotional reactions when you face a challenging situation or a difficult person. Through the self-awareness process, you will learn how to recognize these emotional reactions, how to identify the situations and people that provoke your emotional reactions and discover how your perceptions affect your emotions. During this phase, your key energy will be mindfulness, so that you can consciously observe the actions of your conditioned self in your current life flow.

Phase 2: Understanding Your Life Conditioning

The second phase is about understanding the life conditioning that created your initial persona and finding out how you developed your conditioned self to hide your vulnerability.

After you discover the perceptions that are igniting your emotional reactions, your next step will be to investigate how the situations in your past affected your initial thought patterns and belief systems and created your initial persona. During this second phase of your journey, you will turn your attention to your past to understand how your life conditioning has formed over the years and made you feel vulnerable throughout your life.

A detailed review of your life is now under way. Note that the experiences that have contributed to your life conditioning are not limited to your childhood memories necessarily. Any traumatic or dramatic event, no matter when it happens in your life, can create thought patterns and belief systems that form your initial persona and affect your perceptions. Through the process of understanding, you will dig deeper into the life experiences that created your underlying fears and became a significant part of your initial persona. Your key energy will be self-compassion for your conditioned self and initial persona so that you can deeply understand your life conditioning and empathize with your initial persona.

Phase 3: Expanding Your Boundaries

The third phase of your journey is about expanding your boundaries that had been contracted by your underlying fears.

During this phase, you will learn how to overcome your underlying fears and free yourself from the layers of your life conditioning so that you can expand your boundaries. You will first observe that the intensity of your emotional reaction depends on how vulnerable a situation or person makes you feel. In order to understand your vulnerability, you will draw your attention inward and recognize your underlying fears. You will realize that the defensive actions you take to deal with challenging situations or difficult people are just tools to hide your vulnerability.

In order to overcome your underlying fears and eliminate your vulnerability, you will need to start taking actions that are the opposite of what you have been doing so far. Overriding the actions of your conditioned self will be challenging in the beginning. You need to be courageous. That's why your key energy in this phase is courage. In order to challenge your conditioned self, you need to be able to get out of your comfort zone and make efforts to overcome your underlying fears.

The fourth phase is about building a solid foundation to support your new and expanded boundaries.

Obviously, expanding your boundaries that have been so contracted for so many years is not an easy task. You have diminished your boundaries to stay within your comfort zone. Keeping them expanded will make you feel uncomfortable in the beginning. This feeling of discomfort and uneasiness is natural when you are exploring the unknown. You will need to build a foundation that holds you while you take the necessary steps to overcome your underlying fears and free your initial persona from the reigns of your life conditioning.

In order to build a solid foundation, you will first learn how to ground yourself so that you can short circuit the impact of a perceived attack and observe your initial thought patterns and belief systems that feed your perceptions. Then, you will practice centering by directing your attention inward and getting in touch with your intense emotions. Over time, centering will help you calm your emotions. Once you learn how to center your emotions, you will be able to consciously adjust your actions to find your balance. Your key energy will be groundedness. When you connect with the energy of groundedness, you will feel a solid foundation underneath your feet that will encourage and empower you to take more actions against your underlying fears and hold your ground against the trigger events.

Phase 5: Connecting with Your Inner Power

The fifth phase is about utilizing the foundation you have built in the previous phase to connect with your inner power.

Inner power is the feeling of being grounded and centered with deep calmness in the face of any challenging life situation. In order to feel safer, you will need to continue to conquer your vulnerability. In this phase, you will explore techniques to effectively overcome your underlying fears.

Now that you have expanded your boundaries and can stand on a solid foundation against your underlying fears, you will be able to accept your vulnerability. Acceptance of vulnerability means that you fully and completely accept who your conditioned self and initial persona are. This acceptance will help you connect with your inner power. Through this connection, you will be able to assertively communicate your true thoughts and emotions without feeling intimidated or without taking things personally. Your key energy is inner calmness which naturally arises when you connect with your inner power.

Phase 6: Expressing Your Authentic Self

The sixth phase is about allowing your authentic self to emerge.

This is the phase you have been waiting for. Now that you are connected with your inner power, you can let your authentic self fully show up in your life. During this phase, you will explore ways to express your authentic self with joy, to manifest your new life routine with gratitude, and to spread love and compassion to others with a deeper connection that you haven't felt before.

During this phase, you will learn about what it means to

express your authentic self. You will connect with what comes from your heart. Your inner power will encourage you to fully express your essence and your uniqueness. The moment you start to express your authentic self, the system of life will provide more opportunities to you to bring your essence out.

In this phase, you will start noticing that your life flows much better, providing you with plenty of chances to live joyfully. You will soon connect with gratitude as you notice glimpses of a beautiful shift already manifesting in different areas of your life. Through this noticeable, positive alignment in your life, you will realize that you are on your way to your highest potential. While continuing to travel on your journey as your authentic self, you start to acknowledge others' journeys with love and compassion. Your key energy will be interconnectedness. Living with joy, feeling gratitude and spreading love and compassion will make you notice how connected you are with life and recognize how deeply interconnected we all are with each other.

Phase 7: Stepping into New Beginnings

The seventh and the final phase is about fully activating your authentic self to claim and strengthen its presence for the new life ahead of you.

During this last phase of your journey, you will get ready to step into your new beginnings—new life. As you get in touch with your own innate uniqueness and embrace your new life, you will start to feel less and less vulnerable, and more and more trusting. As you release the mask of your conditioned self, you will start to fully embrace what life has to offer.

In this phase, you will learn how to answer your calling and find your life's work, form fulfilling relationships with love and compassion, and work on your health and well-being. Since the journey within is a life-long process, the new beginnings phase won't be the end of your journey, but a beginning of the beautiful life ahead. Your key energy will be trust. You will trust that everything is in perfect flow. You will realize that life is here to take you even further to deeper joy, abundance, fulfillment and inner calmness. All you need to do is trust life and surrender yourself to the flow of life that will lead you to your highest potential.

Guidelines for Staying on the Journey

When progressing through these phases, you will notice that each step that you take brings a deeper clarity to the meaning of your life. However, this journey is a life-long process and setbacks are not uncommon. You may even experience some resistance when applying the principles of *The Seeker's Manual* to your life. Therefore, carefully study the following guidelines, which will help you stay on course and attain the optimum results on your journey.

Be Patient

The path to your highest potential is not a linear one, even though the individual phases are outlined as above, you may need to go back and forth between the phases to acquire deeper understanding and meaning from each step you take.

Be patient with yourself as you walk slowly through these phases. The best approach is not to expect anything in the beginning.

If you anticipate and expect certain changes too soon in your life and attach yourself to specific outcomes, you may quickly overwhelm yourself. As a result, you will be more likely to quit your journey before you have had the chance to experience the actual positive shift.

With growing awareness of your limiting life patterns, your energy level will continually expand. With deepened understanding of how to break these patterns, the flow of your life will naturally start to improve. The desired changes will eventually start to appear in your life.

This improvement in your life flow happens automatically due to the increase in your energy level. Just understand and accept that your limiting life patterns have been in play for so many years. It will take some time for them to disappear from your life.

Be a patient seeker. Trust yourself and trust life. Everything else will follow.

Own Your Journey: Be Diligent and Self-Disciplined

You will be traveling this journey alone. At times, you may feel that you have little or no support from your loved ones. You may even think that people around you are the source of emotional triggers and therefore hinder your progress. Even though you know that situations and people are in your life for a reason, you may still feel alone and disconnected from everything and everyone around you. You may be tempted to give up and quit your journey. That's when you need diligence more than ever. That's when you intensify your practice, and dig deeper for more energy to stay the course. This kind of journey requires strong, focused dedication and commitment.

The journey within is like climbing a mountain. In the early stages of your journey, you will be in the dark, trying to find your footing on the slopes of the mountain. Climbing all the way up to its summit may seem like a daunting task. Keep practicing the techniques described in this manual diligently and climbing up will become easier. You will soon gain a better perspective of the terrain that you are dealing with. As you connect with the key energy of each phase, your steps on this path will be more comfortable and easier. As you get closer to the peak, you'll start appreciating the beautiful and majestic views the higher altitudes provide.

Remember this is *your* journey. *Your* life. The desire to find full expression of your essence is the driving force behind your diligent work. Your march toward finding your place in this world is under way. This march requires not just diligence, but self-discipline as well. You will notice that the tools, exercises and practices recommended in this manual are not particularly new. Many of them have been practiced for centuries. They are not that difficult or complicated to practice either. Be firm and persistent in applying these principles. Practicing the exercises regularly is essential to seeing the positive effects in your life. Your diligence in understanding and applying them to your life—and the necessity of self-disciplined practice on a regular basis—will be crucial in keeping you on your path.

It is *your* journey, and it is *your* individual empowerment—own it.

As you go deeper on your journey, and acquire more self-knowledge and a better understanding of your life patterns, you will start noticing your thought patterns and belief systems even more. You will realize where and when you drain your energy, and how you lose your connection with your inner power. These moments of insightful realization are perfect opportunities for taking direct actions aimed at breaking your life patterns. You will be encouraged to study this in more detail throughout each phase but, for now, keep in mind that without taking action, it's impossible to break limiting life patterns.

You can't wait for others do the work for you. You can't just expect others to change. You can't ask the situations to change. Sometimes the actions you need to take will go directly against the long time habits and patterns established for years by your life conditioning. As you take actions, your energy expands and sends an important message to life that you are ready to change your life. Through your diligent, patient and determined steps, you announce to the universe that you are ready to find your place in the world and will keep walking on your path until you achieve your highest potential.

Your Experience is Your Only Proof

Each journey is unique, like each of us. No two paths are the same. When you start applying the guidance provided in *The Seeker's Manual,* your energy will expand and you will experience a shift in your life. Simply acknowledge this positive shift. Notice how it keeps re-occurring when you take more actions.

You are the primary witness of your progress on this journey. The evidence of this progress is your experience only. Carefully and consistently study your life experiences and observe your actions, your reactions, your words, your thoughts, and your emotions, so that you can learn about your life conditioning, your initial persona and your conditioned self.

During your journey, you may encounter some resistance both from within and from those around you. You may painfully discover your limiting life patterns that have bound and constrained you for a very long time, in some cases, throughout your life. Breaking them may feel like betraying yourself or your loved ones or people close to you. Even when you feel absolutely trapped in a challenging life situation, or think that life is unfair, or are about to lose hope and fall into despair—*never forget that you have the inner power and innate capacity to improve the flow of your life.*

You opened the door by picking up this manual. Now it is time to walk through that door to embrace your journey and achieve your highest potential.

Keep a Journal

You will come across a lot of insightful experiences during your journey where you will gain a deeper understanding of your life conditioning and who your conditioned self and initial persona are. Keep a journal to record these insights so that you can use this self-knowledge for the subsequent phases of your journey. In addition to keeping notes of your experiences and accumulating your observations in one place, documenting your thoughts has a very powerful energy that magically facilitates more comprehensive self-knowledge and reflection. Often, you will notice that writing will provide an interesting new perspective about your life experiences that you had not noticed before.

Some of you may find writing your thoughts and emotions down challenging. If that's the case, try to take brief mental notes of how your state of mind is at certain moments. Alternatively, you can try to write down key words or short phrases, instead of long narratives.

Note that this is not a diary, but a life conditioning journal. Therefore, the focus should be on your thoughts and emotions, and not on others. Following is a set of brief examples of how this type of journaling works.

"This morning when I was rushing to my nine o'clock meeting, I kept falling behind the slowest drivers on the freeway. I was getting very frustrated because I thought they were going to make me even later for my meeting. During the meeting, I couldn't concentrate much because I was exhausted from the anger I felt towards these drivers. I really don't understand why they drive so slowly in the fast lane."

"During the afternoon of that day, I had a presentation. During the presentation, my boss heavily criticized some of the slides that I had prepared. I felt very low and also furious that my boss chose to do the bashing in front of my team. I felt his comments were very unfair. Does he recognize that I worked on these slides until midnight?"

"When I came home that day, I was feeling exhausted. I still had the unfair comments of my boss in my head. I also realized that I was very sensitive at dinner. Every comment my spouse

made frustrated me. Why am I taking things too personally? What is it that bothers me so much? Feeling tired and depleted, I went to bed. "

As you can see from above examples, the life conditioning journaling is an internal account of what's going on in your head, as opposed to what's happening in your life. The focus is on your emotional reactions. It will force you to pay attention to your thoughts and emotions in every situation. Over time, as you add more tools and receive more guidance from *The Seeker's Manual*, you will be able to objectively analyze the situations and write down deeper insights into why you display certain emotional reactions.

While observing and witnessing your conditioned self and noticing the vulnerability of your initial persona in your daily routine, you get a chance to gather lot of information about your life conditioning. This type of journaling helps you capture this self-knowledge and ask insightful questions about your life and who you are. Instead of dealing with these questions in your head, by writing them down, you will be able to connect the dots between your limiting life patterns and your intense emotional reactions. You will soon see the pieces of your life conditioning puzzle coming together in your journals.

Connect Energetically

A journey of this magnitude requires not only mental commitment or diligent actions, but also a deep connection with the specific energy level that each phase provides. Therefore, do not just practice the principles of the journey and its phases, but also try to feel the exact energy that each phase helps you connect with. This concept may not be familiar to you. It is also difficult to comprehend. However, as long as you do the key practices diligently on a regular basis and carefully apply the concepts and the principles of this manual, you will connect with the specific energy level of each particular phase.

Now, check in with yourself. How committed are you to embark on a journey to discover the meaning of your life and achieve your highest potential? Do you feel a strong, persistent determination that will carry you throughout your journey? What is the quality of your commitment? What is the firmness of your purpose to transform your life to a better flow where you will feel joy, fulfillment and inner calmness?

If you are ready, let's take the first step towards achieving your highest potential: Becoming Self-Aware.

3 · Becoming Self-Aware

A SELF-REALIZATION journey is all about honoring your life's purpose, which is getting to know who you are—first your conditioned self, then your initial persona and finally your emerging authentic self. Therefore, becoming aware of your conditioned self—who you are now, how you feel, how you see the world, what matters to you—is the perfect starting point for your journey. During the process of getting to know your conditioned self, you will also gradually become aware of your initial persona and your life conditioning and observe how your conditioned self chooses to react when facing limiting life patterns.

Life, by design, is very generous when it comes to providing opportunities to practice becoming self-aware. These opportunities are happening in your life right now. They appear as limiting life patterns. Since your conditioned thought patterns and belief systems are deeply ingrained within your energy body, you can observe them in your actions at all times and in every aspect of your life.

Until now, you didn't quite know how to utilize these situations to become aware of your conditioned self. You have made the mistake of directing your attention outward, and often, blamed others or circumstances. Meanwhile, you have missed opportunities to get to know your conditioned self. Your attention needs to be constantly directed inwards. The answers are within you!

Anatomy of a Life Pattern

In order to utilize the opportunity provided by a life pattern, you first need to understand what a life pattern is comprised of. Let's break it down into its individual components so you have a clear picture of what a life pattern looks like:

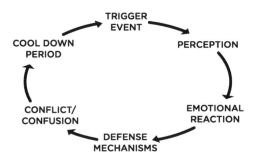

Illustration 4. Anatomy of a Life Pattern

Every life pattern starts with a trigger event. Based on your perceptions, you interpret the trigger event to be a threat or an attack to your conditioned self. Due to this interpretation, you feel vulnerable and take the trigger event personally. You then emotionally react to protect your conditioned self's image and disguise your initial persona. Your intense emotions immediately launch your defense mechanisms to cover your vulnerability and ward off the threatening appearance of a trigger event. In order to defend your conditioned self, you exert a lot of energy, thus lower your energy level.

When your energy level is low, your fears get magnified and you find yourself experiencing a period of conflict and confusion, which usually involves arguments, heated discussions and distorted perceptions where you question your life choices about your spouse, work, boss, friends. Time slowly passes and the emotional effects of the trigger event loses its intensity—most of us say "time heals", but actually, in a futile effort to forget the pain and suffering, you bury your underlying fears further down into your energy blockages. You don't want to face your initial persona and your vulnerability. You just want to move on.

Things seem to finally cool down a bit. You start to forget the trigger event, put your mask of your conditioned self back on, and continue with your current life flow. This cooling-off period lasts for a short while, until the next trigger event kicks off another life pattern where your conditioned self feels attacked—again.

Nobody is exempt from limiting life patterns. The system of life provides them to everyone who has underlying fears and related energy blockages. At the same time, being part of the same system, we all have the capacity to break our life patterns. One of the most probable reasons you are holding this manual in your hands is that you have had enough of your limiting life patterns. You want things to change, but you don't know what to change exactly and you don't know how.

The reason why you are stuck in experiencing your limiting life patterns over and over again is that your energy vibrates at a low frequency. You keep draining your energy to defend your conditioned self and hide your vulnerability. Your energy level stays low. On those low energy levels, you don't have access to your inner power to make any permanent changes to your routine. Your life becomes stagnant. Everything stays the same.

To break the stagnancy and get rid of limiting life patterns, you need to raise your energy level. You can only raise your energy level by releasing your energy blockages, as they bring your energy level down. You can release them by understanding your life conditioning and getting in touch with your repressed thoughts and emotions. In order to deepen your understanding of your life conditioning, you need to be able to get to know your conditioned self and initial persona by observing their actions in your limiting life patterns. For this observation to be effective, you need to increase your self-awareness.

Self-Awareness Process

The self-awareness process is the method that helps you gain deeper insights into each component of a life pattern so that you can see your conditioned self in action. By digging into the depths of what makes up a life pattern, you will acquire the valuable self-knowledge you need. This process is the key to unlocking the stagnant energy that keeps you within your life patterns. Once you start becoming aware of your conditioned self and your initial persona, your energy level naturally increases. At a higher energy level, you feel more powerful to take a conscious action that can overcome your underlying fears, release your energy blockages and break your limiting life patterns.

When you apply the self-awareness process to your life, you will realize that seemingly unrelated situations and people tend to provoke the same emotional reactions in you. As a matter of fact, your intense emotional reactions are the common denominator among your limiting life patterns. Even though the trigger events may look like entirely different situations or people, your intense emotional reactions display similar characteristics when these events cause you to feel vulnerable and when you take situations personally.

As long as you maintain the mask of your conditioned self to disguise your initial persona, you will live vulnerably under the influence of your life conditioning. As a result, you will feel, say, not good enough, and will have the same intense emotional reaction to situations whether you receive a judgmental comment from your boss, get a question from your spouse in a control-ling tone, or notice the dissatisfaction of your parents on their faces. As mentioned earlier, note that even though feeling not good enough is a very common initial thought pattern and belief system, you may have other underlying fears that are unique to your own life experiences. Therefore, while reading the examples in this manual, apply them to your specific circumstances and replace not good enough with not lovable, not worthy, not rec-ognized, not successful or any other initial thought pattern and belief system that your initial persona might have.

Recognizing Your Intense Emotional Reactions

Even though a trigger event is what kicks off a life pattern, you don't notice it until you feel an intense emotion. That's why you will need to start your self-awareness process by recognizing your intense emotional reactions, instead of identifying your trigger events. You notice your emotions first because you experience life through emotions. Have you noticed that the memories you vividly remember have a significant, positive or negative, emotional impact on you? You would remember every detail of what you were doing at the time when you heard shocking news on the radio or received a tragic phone call about a family member. You relate to trigger events only through how they make you feel.

From here on, whenever you take a situation personally or whenever someone pushes your buttons, observe your intense emotional reactions. Try to connect with them exactly when you feel them. Just notice them as they arise within you. Whether it is anger, frustration, anxiety, sadness, jealousy, guilt, grief or any other emotion, simply recognize what you feel, when you feel it. Even though your intense emotional reactions are so natural, you may find it too painful to connect with them and to face them. Don't judge your emotions. Don't feel guilty or shameful about feeling certain emotions. Simply take note of it.

There is one issue though. Due to the energetic wiring, the time that lapses from the moment you experience the trigger event to the moment you feel your intense emotion is very short. Before you know it, your emotions overwhelm you. If you want to observe your conditioned self in your life patterns and recognize what your conditioned self really feels, you need to prolong your intense emotional reaction.

Prolonging your reaction is easier said than done. However, it is one of the most important tools in the self-awareness process. Here is how it's done. First, be very alert when your emotional reaction bubbles up. Right at that time, you will need to take a step back from the situation and observe your conditioned self from a distance. Then, connect with the emotions that you feel at that very moment. Even though it will be very difficult to do this in the beginning, diligently work on creating a space between the trigger event and your emotional reactions. The key practice for this phase is self-observation meditation. By practicing this technique, you will start experiencing a brief gap before you emotionally react to trigger events.

Creating that space will allow you to delay the launch of your defense mechanisms and, therefore, allow you to consciously witness what's going on within you and why you feel like defending your conditioned self. The trick is to stay with your intense emotions without acting on them. Feel the anger, frustration, anxiety, sadness, jealousy, guilt, grief or any other emotion as long as you can, until you thoroughly acknowledge them. Any time you feel an intense emotion, write it down in your journal.

Identifying Your Trigger Events

A trigger event is an event that sets a course of action in motion. On your journey, a trigger event is a circumstance that ignites an emotional reaction in you. The trigger event may include a specific situation, a particular person, an attitude, a word, a scene, or any other circumstance that provokes your thoughts and emotions. Even though trigger events come from outside, note that the self-awareness process is internal. Eventually, you will care less about the trigger events and focus more on your intense emotional reactions.

Everybody experiences their trigger events differently. The way you respond to a trigger event is based on how vulnerable you feel. Remember that when something or someone pushes your buttons, it means that you have an energy blockage you need to be aware of and eventually deal with. In other words, trigger events are very personal. How personal it is can be observed when you complain about your trigger events to others. You will notice that they often don't quite understand what your complaint is about. They often see a simpler version of what you describe or offer quick and obvious solutions to you or don't think it is a big deal.

In order to approach a trigger event objectively, look inside and analyze the trigger event through your own emotions, not through certain outside circumstances or attitudes of others. Then, describe the trigger event. Write down in your journal how a particular event triggered your intense emotional reactions.

Discovering Your Perceptions

You take trigger events personally, because your perceptions tell you to. Behind every perception, there is a thought pattern and a belief system. Your life conditioning constantly feeds your perceptions and gives meaning to your life experiences. Your perceptions dictate exactly how you should interpret a life situation or someone's attitude. When experiencing a situation, you immediately label and categorize that information per your life conditioning and feel that you need to defend your conditioned self and disguise your initial persona. You respond to it according to this interpretation.

Have you had experiences where you initially perceived a situation one way but then later on evidence showed you another perspective? For example, you may have thought that your boss didn't trust you or didn't like your work, but later on, found out that you were assigned to an important project? Or maybe you had moments where you had serious doubts about your relationship and thought that your spouse did not love you anymore, but later on, noticed that they made a thoughtful gesture or gave you heartfelt loving support while you were experiencing a difficult period in your life.

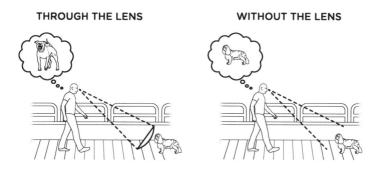

Illustration 5. Mistaking a Spaniel for a Pit bull

You don't typically change your perceptions throughout life, unless you proactively choose to do so. They are the lenses through which you look at life and protect your conditioned self. Suppose you had a bad encounter with a pit bull previously. As a result of that incident, you developed a fear of dogs. Now your thought patterns and belief systems, which feed your perceptions may tell you that all dogs are dangerous. Therefore, your perceptions will always alert you whenever a possible encounter with a dog exists. Looking through the lens of your perceptions, you may mistake a spaniel for a pit bull.

When you don't question your initial thought patterns and belief systems, you keep responding to life situations through the lens of your perceptions. You may label your boss as a micro manager and then, perceive their comments as micromanagement. You may label your spouse as stingy, and then, ignore their generous manners.

The purpose of your perceptions is to protect your conditioned self from any possible threat. The issue is that you may perceive some of the situations and people as a threat when in reality they are not. Since you respond to them according to how you perceive them, you drain your energy unnecessarily and stay at a low energy level.

In order to work on your perceptions, you need to deepen your self-awareness and figure out the footprints of your life conditioning and how this impacts your response to life situations and people. Through the self-awareness process, you will be able to discover your perceptions and open your energy up to deeper insights. By becoming more aware of your conditioned self, you will be able to take steps to defuse the strong hold of your perceptions over your actions and change your conditioned response to trigger events.

Write down in your journal the details of the initial thought patterns and belief systems that feed your perceptions. Also, acknowledge the specific response you give to trigger events based on your perceptions.

Life Pattern Components in a Real-Life Scenario

You have your own unique life experiences that you will need to observe and learn from so that you can reach your highest potential. Guidance is helpful to show you the steps that you can take to attain higher energy levels, but at the same time, guidance needs to be applied and tested in real life scenarios. Throughout *The Seeker's Manual*, you will read some possible scenarios and examples where you will get to see how the guidance is applied to life. While processing these examples, try to visualize how the essence of the hypothetical scenario applies to your life. While reviewing your own specific life situations, try to solve the puzzle of your own life conditioning and unmask your conditioned self.

Let's say that you get frustrated every time your partner doesn't seem to be listening to you. This partner might be your spouse, boy/girlfriend, coworker, boss, friend, sibling and others, who would trigger your intense emotional reactions so that you could become aware of your conditioned self and learn about your life conditioning.

So, your partner doesn't seem to be listening to you. They seem to be distant and aloof when you are excited to talk about something that you find interesting. You feel that your partner is not interested in what you have to say. In addition, from time to time, they might use a degrading tone when responding to your questions or comments. As a result, over time, you stop wanting to share anything with them. Why should you? Every time you talk about something, you know your partner will not be interested. They always ignore you and treat you as if you are not important. You keep getting frustrated and angry with them, but you don't know what to do.

Even though you want to avoid being ignored, situations will occur where your partner finds a way to ignore you and make you feel unimportant. When you are in a limiting life pattern like this, your intentions won't be able to change the situation and the trigger events you are exposed to. Feeling helpless and powerless, you may decide to distance yourself from your partner and question whether the relationship is worth continuing.

Before you make any major decisions though, let's go through the self-awareness process and identify the components of this particular life pattern.

Remember, whenever you have an intense emotional reaction, you need to use it as an opportunity to become aware of your conditioned self. Start your self-awareness process by reviewing your emotions. What is your intense emotional reaction? Is it anger or frustration? Whatever it is, notice it, write it down in your journal. Just connect with your emotions as they come up. Without self-judgment or self-blame for any of these feelings, just notice what is coming up.

The next question is: what is your trigger? At your initial observation, it may seem like it is your partner who has caused these intense emotions. But, what really triggers your emotional reaction is their disregard of what you are saying. It is important to identify your exact trigger. If you blame your partner for ignoring you, then you won't be able to expand your awareness and get to know your conditioned self. Thus, the trigger is not your partner. In this particular case, the trigger is being ignored or not being respected. This identification is very important because people and situations will change, but whenever you feel ignored, you will show the same exact intense emotional reaction.

The next step is to discover your perceptions: How did you perceive this situation? Here again, the focus is on you, not on your partner. Your perception may be that they always disregard you. Your perception may have already labeled them and put them in a box. Whenever you try to talk about something you *know* that your partner will ignore you. But wait a second! You have been blaming them for a while, but has anything changed? So this time, instead of blaming, dig deeper to understand what's really going on inside your mind.

Initially, you might resist this guidance and think, "But, my partner causes me to feel that way!" Again, it's not what they do, but how you perceive what they do. After all, you can't change your partner or the way they interact with you. You can only discover your perceptions and understand why you feel vulnerable. By internally working on your vulnerability, you can learn more about yourself and your life conditioning and eventually change the dynamics within your relationship.

When you decide to look at your perceptions, you may notice that even though you feel not important initially, deep down there might be other thoughts and beliefs that are being triggered as well—you think and believe that you are being not valued, not liked or not loved. Maybe you feel that your partner is abandoning you by treating you so indifferently. During your self-awareness process, it is important to go deeper into your perceptions until you articulate the exact thought patterns and belief systems that resonate with your unique life experiences.

The self-awareness process is very powerful and transformative, but at the same time, difficult to go through. You may face internal resistance. You may feel that you are exposing your initial persona too much when you dig into your life conditioning and observe your conditioned self's intense emotions. You may want to do things the old way. Be patient with the process. Take small steps to bring a little more self-awareness into your life.

At this phase of your journey, you simply need to work on

your conditioned self. That's it. Just recognize your intense emotional reactions, identify your trigger events and discover your perceptions. You will soon notice that this self-awareness will naturally raise your energy level. As a result, you will gradually change the way you respond to situations and people. And magically—actually, due to the shift in your energy level—situations will change and people will interact with you differently. That is how beautiful the system of life is. You are absolutely in charge! You control the flow of your life. You change and everything around you changes accordingly—naturally.

Key Energy: Mindfulness

Mindfulness means to be aware of what's happening. In order to test your mindfulness, try to notice how aware you are when you're driving, listening to music, talking to a friend or writing an email. Do you pay attention to what's going on? Do you notice your thoughts or do you find yourself daydreaming and jumping from one thought to another?

When you are lost in thought, applying self-awareness process to your life will be challenging. Therefore, connecting with the energy of mindfulness is very important.

Through mindfulness, you can gain access to the deeper understanding you need for deciphering your life conditioning and getting to know your conditioned self. To connect with the energy of mindfulness, you first need to stop living unconsciously, based on your energetic wiring—the way you conditioned yourself.

Instead, you need to start living consciously and learn to be in the present moment with heightened awareness of your own thoughts and emotions. Observe your life with this alert attention as each moment unfolds. Witness yourself, others, and situations from a distance with detachment and indifference. Yet intimately notice everything that is happening in your life, and within your mind, in any given moment.

To deeply connect with the energy of mindfulness and to stay present in every situation, you need to be able to practice self-observation.

Key Practice: Self-Observation Meditation

Self-observation meditation is a mental training tool that improves your ability to step back from a situation and witness it from a distance. If you consistently practice this meditation technique, you will be able to observe your thoughts and emotions, as well as the actions of your conditioned self in any given moment.

When you can step out of a situation, you will be able to detach yourself from your thoughts and emotions. As a result, they will not be able to pull you into the chaos happening in your busy mind. You remain outside of your mind's activity and stay alert to what's going on around you. Consequently, you can easily bring the energy of mindfulness into whatever you do, say, think and feel. Only then will you gain deeper insights into the actions of your conditioned self. Self-observation meditation is THE most important practice that you will be performing throughout your journey. Therefore, allocate time to this meditation on a daily basis.

Meditation is not a relaxation practice; it's a mental training of reaching a quiet, yet observant state of mind so that you can witness your thoughts and emotions from a distance. Through diligent practice of self-observation meditation, you will get into a habit of keeping your mind calm, alert, undisturbed, detached and indifferent even when facing challenging life situations or difficult people.

Before you start your self-observation meditation, here is another tip. In order to incorporate a meditation practice in your daily routine, you first need to look at how your day flows. Instead of focusing on what time you should meditate, focus on where in your daily routine you can meditate. Will it be easier right after you wake up or right before you leave the house or when you come home from a busy day or right before you go to bed? Try different alternatives until you settle on one routine. Then, incorporate it into your day on a consistent basis. After meditating for a few weeks, test whether your practice brings more awareness to your life. Do you notice a difference on the days that you meditate? How is the flow of life on those days that you don't meditate? Pay attention to the correlation between your meditation practice and how your day goes.

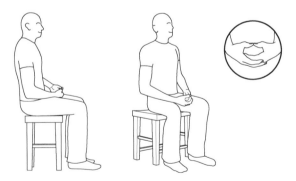

Illustration 6. Self-Observation Meditation

Let's get started. First, pick a location where you won't be interrupted for the duration of your practice. As a beginner, I suggest you start with a three-minute practice. You can add more minutes later on when you feel more comfortable with the process.

To start your practice, sit on a comfortable chair with knees at a ninety-degree angle and your feet flat on the floor. Your back, neck and head are straight. If the chair has a back, move forward towards the center of the chair, so that your back doesn't rest on the chair. If you have to lean your back on the chair, that's okay too, but still keep your back straight. Relax your body and maintain this posture without becoming too rigid or strained.

Now, put your hands on your lap, facing up. Then, connect your thumbs on top of your palms while fingers are aligned on top of each other. Thumbs should be barely touching each other. With your arms relaxed, thumbs lightly touching, take a deep breath in, and when exhaling close your eyes. Place your tongue gently on the roof of your mouth and put the tip of your tongue behind your front teeth. Keep your mouth closed, breathing naturally.

Start concentrating on your thumbs. Focus on that tangible feeling where your thumbs touch each other. While trying to keep your focus on your thumbs, gently observe the thoughts and images that are going through your mind. Whenever you find yourself deep in your thoughts, bring your attention back to your thumbs. Notice your thoughts without reacting. Notice the images with a calm indifference and detachment. Keep your focus on your thumbs.

In the beginning, you will constantly find yourself pulled by your thoughts. One thought after another will take you away from your concentration and lead you into different memories, past regrets, future worries. Whenever you find yourself distracted and wandering through your thoughts, ask yourself, "What am I thinking right now?" This question will create a brief moment, where you will be able to distance yourself from your thoughts, become again the witness of your thoughts and then, patiently and diligently bring your focus back to your thumbs.

Observe this tug of war between your mind chatter and your concentration. The goal is to keep your attention on your thumbs for longer periods of time. But don't get frustrated when you can't hold your focus for more than a few seconds at a time. That is okay. In the beginning, or maybe even after months of training, it may still be difficult to overcome the mind chatter and find the still place between you and your thoughts. Don't give up. Keep allocating time on a daily basis and practice diligently.

To finish your practice, take a deep breath and exhale slowly. Then, open your eyes and release your hands and thumbs. Sit quietly for a minute or two to reflect on the repeating thoughts and images you encountered during your practice.

As a daily practice, I recommend that you practice this meditation every morning right after you wake up—before eating anything. If you would like, you can repeat the same meditation for three minutes before you go to bed every night. When you feel comfortable with this meditation technique, add more minutes to your practice and do it at different times throughout your day.

4 · Understanding Your Life Conditioning

BECOMING AWARE of your conditioned self was all about mind-fully noticing your life conditioning in your current life flow. While observing your life today, you started connecting the dots between your intense emotional reactions and your perceptions that feed them. You started getting glimpses of your conditioned self in action.

Now, understanding your life conditioning will be all about exploring your past and reviewing the events that made you feel vulnerable and created your initial persona. Through the process of understanding, you will realize how different situations in your past affected your initial thought patterns and belief systems and created your underlying fears. By looking deeper into your fears, you will begin to understand exactly how your life conditioning has become ingrained within your energy body.

Process of Understanding

The process of understanding starts with recognizing the events that caused you to repress your thoughts and emotions. You need to understand these events as they provide information about your energy blockages. In order to gain a deeper understanding of your life conditioning, you will need to look at situations from your past and also at people who played an important role in each and every situation. Once you start acquiring some insights into how you formed your initial thought patterns and belief systems, you will understand what really happened and how certain experiences have formed your initial persona, for example, thinking and believing that you are not good enough and how you then conditioned yourself to act and live to hide your vulnerability, for example, fear of others perceiving you as not good enough.

While reviewing the traumatic and emotionally impactful events of your past, it may be very difficult to isolate yourself from the situations and people. The past doesn't necessarily mean your childhood, but rather any event in the past that brought out an intense emotion in you. To thoroughly understand what went on in these past experiences, you need to take a step back and observe those particular situations. While observing, focus only on yourself—your thoughts and emotions. You need to become an objective witness to those particular experiences so that you can access the initial thought patterns, belief systems and intense emotions that you felt at that time. Similar to observation of your conditioned self that you practiced during the Becoming Self-Aware phase, apply a certain objectivity, detachment and curiosity to the review of your past. Just observe and acknowledge how key life experiences formed your initial persona, for example, interpreting your parents' attitude and thinking and believing that whatever you accomplished was never good enough for your parents.

Looking at your past may remind you of some decisions that you regret. You could also bump into old memories that you didn't want to face. If you start to "re-live" these incidents with the same emotional intensity that you initially experienced, you won't be able to sustain your witness status. You will get deeply and emotionally involved. You will want to push your initial thoughts and emotions back down into your energy blockages. This defensive action is very natural and understandable. But, remember that you can only move forward by releasing your energy blockages. Your progression into a better life goes through healing the old wounds. So try to be patient during this process.

While objectively examining your past, realize how vulnerable you felt during these traumatic experiences. Remember that you repressed your thoughts and emotions because you felt vulnerable. If you feel ready, turn your focus to your vulnerability. Dig deeper into your life experiences and look at the key relationships and key life situations that had an impact on your thoughts and emotions. Observe your vulnerability in these instances. Notice it. Acknowledge it. Understand it. Embrace it.

Let's say, growing up, your parents' relationship was rocky. They constantly argued in front of you. No day passed without them blaming and demeaning each other. Suppose they finally got divorced. At the time, you felt deep down that their break up was your fault. You thought you should have saved their relationship, but couldn't. You felt guilty. You wanted to save their relationship. You wanted to make them happy but your efforts were in vain. You felt lonely. You thought that they abandoned you. You believed that they did not love you.

While looking at these events in your past and going through your initial thoughts and emotions, recognize how vulnerable you felt back then. Observe how your life experiences conditioned your initial persona. Realize how your initial persona started to fear that you were not lovable and that people would abandon you and that you would be lonely forever. You felt extremely vulnerable, but your initial persona didn't have the power to overcome these fears.

When you developed your conditioned self and disguised your initial persona, you buried your underlying fears along with your initial thought patterns and belief systems into your energy blockages. They stayed within your energy body covered for the rest of your life. Today, they remain concealed underneath your energy blockages. In order to release your energy blockages and break your limiting life patterns, you need to face your vulnerability and your underlying fears.

Underlying Fears

You have done enough defending so far in your life. Time has come to understand why you defend your conditioned self and why you are always on guard.

Yet again, your self-observation practice comes in very handy here. The ability to take a step back from the situation and observe it from a distance will give you a chance to interrupt the energetically wired initial thought patterns and belief systems and recognize your underlying fears.

The following is a brief overview of the most common fears. The list is not all-inclusive and meant to highlight some of the fears most of us deal with on a daily basis. While going through the examples, think about your life situation and accurately identify your own underlying fears.

If your initial persona has fear of not being good enough, then you may have developed your conditioned self as someone who is a perfectionist to avoid any possibility of being seen as not good enough. Under the mask of your conditioned self, you may always want to excel in whatever you do. Instead of enjoying simple things, you may turn everything you do into a task. The trigger events that may push your buttons will be situations and people who challenge your ideas and thoughts, and treat you as not good enough. Every criticism may hurt you and make you feel vulnerable, as you work so hard to be perfect.

At work, even though you are recognized by some of your colleagues, you may feel that it's not enough. As a result, you aggressively force your conditioned self to accomplish more things. You may work until you exhaust yourself and still feel that you are not doing enough work or not getting enough praise. In relationships, the trigger events may occur when your partner questions your actions or provides suggestions. On the other hand, you may feel that whatever you do for your partner, your efforts are not appreciated. You feel not good enough for them. Observe your life patterns, do you experience fear of not being good enough?

Fear of Abandonment

If your initial persona has fear of abandonment, then you may have developed your conditioned self as someone who withdraws from people or has a hard time trusting them. You may find yourself going to great lengths to establish deeper, but fewer relationships. You may surround yourself with a few trustworthy friends or family members. Even though you may run away from situations where there is a possibility of being abandoned, life patterns always bring you the trigger events that poke at your vulnerability—fear of abandonment.

At work, even though you struggle to establish warm relationships, you may not quite connect with your boss or coworkers, or often feel outside of the clique. You may have one close colleague, a confidant with whom you share your thoughts and emotions. In relationships, you may choose partners who seem to be traveling a lot or are emotionally unavailable or noncommittal. Even though you fight hard for their attention, they may seem to be narcissistic and self-centered. Observe your life patterns, do you experience fear of abandonment?

Fear of Failure

If your initial persona has fear of failure, then you may have developed your conditioned self as someone who procrastinates on projects and finds excuses to delay them. You may even sabotage your efforts by giving your attention to other things or wasting your time with details, so that the project doesn't progress to a completion where you could attain results. Of course, your limiting life patterns won't leave you alone and will consistently push you into situations where you feel like a failure.

You may be a business owner getting ready to launch your company and find yourself doing tedious side projects rather than focusing on the core steps necessary to launch your company. You may have self-doubts about your ability to run a business. You may constantly seek approval from your family and friends.

You may require lot of encouragement to continue with your venture. You may feel uncomfortable if you do something that is outside of their expectations. Observe your life patterns, do you experience fear of failure?

Fear of Rejection

If your initial persona has a fear of being rejected, then you may have developed your conditioned self as someone who wants to please people and accommodate them and place their needs above everything else so that you feel included and accepted. Within the fear of rejection, there is also an element of fear of worthlessness, where you assign your self-worth on how much love and attention you receive from others.

At work, you may find it difficult to say no to people. As a result, you may take on more projects than you can handle. You may stay late or often skip lunch to get things done. In relationships, you may be extremely codependent, constantly looking for affirmations of love from your partner. You may choose to extend your care giving and help to the point of exhaustion as you place others' needs above your own. You may make the relationship more important to you than you are to yourself. Observe your life patterns, do you experience fear of rejection?

Fear of Loneliness

If your initial persona has fear of loneliness, then, you may have developed your conditioned self as someone who wants to meet and stay in touch with as many people as possible. You may like socializing, networking and organizing events to bring people together. You may also want to meet and connect with people on every occasion as much as you can. However, the trigger event in these life patterns may be that you are unable to establish deep connections with people, so that you always feel lonely, even though surrounded by a lot of people. The lack of connection will always make you uneasy, and force you to make more connections in an unsuccessful effort to avoid loneliness. Observe your life patterns, do you experience fear of loneliness?

Identifying your Underlying Fears

While going through the list of common fears above, have you identified yours? If so, describe your underlying fears. Be very specific.

Then, do you recognize your conditioned self? Can you observe the actions of your conditioned self in the challenging life situations that you are dealing with right now?

And, finally, do you associate yourself with the underlying fears of your initial persona? Review the events from your past that created your initial persona. Understand how your initial thought patterns and belief systems affect your actions and how your life conditioning influences the way you see the world today.

Just notice how your initial thought patterns and belief systems have formed your underlying fears and how you have developed your conditioned self as a mask to hide your vulnerability.

No matter what identity your conditioned self has taken on, it is only whomever you have decided to create under the circumstances. You can't see it as good or bad. It's a protection mechanism or a mask that you have chosen in order to hide behind. Keep in mind that you have created this protection to survive and feel safe. So be gentle and kind with yourself while uncovering your underlying fears and getting to know your conditioned self and initial persona. Try to understand where these identities come from, without self-judgment and without blaming others.

Throughout your life, you keep switching back and forth between these two identities. Your first identity, initial persona, constantly stays at the vulnerable state of mind that is governed by your initial thought patterns and belief systems, such as, "I'm not good enough", "I'm not lovable". As your vulnerability brings out your underlying fears, the second identity, your conditioned self comes alive and says, "I'm good enough, I'm perfect" or "People love me."

While swinging between these identities, you ignore your underlying fears by repressing your true thoughts and emotions even more. As a result, your energy blockages stay intact and keep attracting your limiting life patterns, which expose the exact underlying fear that you are trying to run away from. You project your thoughts and beliefs onto situations and people. Then, like a mirror, life keeps reflecting back to you what you don't want to experience.

Illustration 7. "I'm not Good Enough"

Whenever you feel vulnerable, pay attention to your initial thought patterns and belief systems that have created your underlying fears. Notice how you project them onto others. Whenever you think and believe that you are not good enough, sooner or later, someone or something will echo your thoughts and beliefs and provoke that fear in you. It's like as if you project your underlying fears onto situations and people and they, like mirrors, reflect them back to you. Therefore, you can't escape from your fears; you must overcome them to raise your energy level so that you can achieve your highest potential. What a brilliant system!

It may be difficult and challenging at times to feel that the system of life is on your side. Once you start to overcome your underlying fears and free yourself from the layers of your life conditioning, you will have a deeper appreciation for this system. So, now, let's explore your current life situation and prove that what you are experiencing today carries a lot of clues about your underlying fears. In a sense, life is offering valuable information for you to understand so that you can liberate your conditioned self and initial persona. To decode this information, you need to learn how to conduct an internal investigation.

Conducting an Internal Investigation

An internal investigation is simply asking a series of why questions to dig deeper into the layers of your life conditioning—your initial thought patterns and belief systems—in order to identify what your underlying fears are. The best time to launch an internal investigation is when you experience a limiting life pattern and show an intense emotional reaction to a trigger event.

While going through your internal investigation, be curious about where each answer will lead you. The purpose of *why* is not to point fingers at yourself or accusing yourself for feeling certain emotions. The spirit of *why* is to get a meaningful insight into a particular underlying fear buried underneath your energy blockages. Therefore, be patient and stick to your questions and answers, until you face your underlying fear.

To demonstrate how an internal investigation is conducted, let's go over a hypothetical scenario.

Suppose that you feel completely stuck in your life, where the only thing you do is to go to work, then back home, take care of your kids and spend some time with your spouse. You have no time to do anything else. You feel trapped within this monotonous routine, and don't know how to get out. You complain that you don't enjoy your life anymore. Since you lack enjoyment in your life and feel stuck, you find comfort in other things. You may have gained weight or started drinking more or found yourself watching TV most of the time. Since you are not happy about the way things are, you get easily agitated and frustrated. You snap quickly.

Now let's conduct an internal investigation and find out what's going on in this limiting life pattern. Following are some example questions and possible answers that you may use as part of your internal investigation. Notice how a statement in the answer, noted in italics, gets turned into a question to further the investigation deeper into your underlying fears and life conditioning. In the above scenario, you seem to be frustrated. So let's start there:

Why am I frustrated?

- These people always push my buttons. I don't seem to get out of these situations. I don't like them. I don't like the way things flow. *I don't like my life.*

Why don't I like my life?

- I feel trapped. I don't know what to do. I seem to be drifting from one place to another. I don't even remember when I had any personal time for myself. All I do is work for my boss, provide for my family, put my spouse's needs above mine and look after my kids. I can't breathe. *I don't have any personal time.*

Why don't I have any personal time?

- Things are overwhelming. I give. I give. I give. I run from one problem to another. *I don't seem to find time for myself.*

> **Why can't I find time for myself?**
>
> - I have so many responsibilities, I don't even think about myself. *I have to attend to others.*
>
> **Why do I have to attend others?**
>
> - I feel like they need me. *I need to be there for them.*

At this point, you may realize that, throughout your life, you have put others' happiness and needs before your own. You have conditioned yourself to do so. Once you recognize your life conditioning, you are very close to identify your underlying fears that you have been running away from.

Now, continue with your internal investigation.

> **Why do I need to be there for them?**
>
> - If I'm not there for them, I'm afraid, they will be unhappy. Then, they will not love me. Then, they will leave me.

The internal investigation will always lead you to a worst-case scenario that you want to avoid. In this situation, the worst-case scenario would be that your family or your boss doesn't need you. They will leave you. If that happened, you would feel worthless, which is exactly what you are afraid of. Due to this underlying fear, you feel safer when others need you. In your conditioned self's mind, if you try to make everybody happy, they will need you. But, you are so focused on ensuring the well-being of others, you ignore your own and find yourself trapped within this limiting life pattern.

Of course, you should not stop making others happy. You do care for people and genuinely help them when they need you. However, there should be a balance in your actions so that you can break your limiting life pattern and at the same time, allocate some personal time to yourself and enjoy your life. You will soon learn about how to balance your actions while overcoming your fears. But for now, let's continue with the internal investigation.

At this stage of your internal investigation, your next step is to go back and review your past and understand how this underlying fear has formed early on in your life. A possible life scenario might have been that you were the oldest sibling and had to take care of your parents and younger siblings, or maybe your parents always asked for your help, and the only way you felt worthy or got attention from them was to please them. Whatever your particular situation might have been, it provided you a framework that helped you feel worthy and loved.

Everybody experiences life differently. Therefore, everyone has their own unique underlying fears and life conditioning. So let's explore the above scenario from a different angle. While reviewing this new thread of another internal investigation, notice how a new series of *why* questions may lead you to a different conclusion.

To explore this new internal investigation path, let's start from the third question in the above scenario, "Why don't I have any personal time?" This time, you may answer it differently, like, "I don't have anything to do in my personal time. *I don't have anything joyful to do.* I don't know what joy is anymore." Then your internal investigation could go deeper, towards a totally different direction, as follows:

> **Why don't I have anything joyful to do?**
>
> - I don't connect with any joyful activity so *I don't like doing anything.*
>
> **Why don't I like doing anything?**
>
> - *It takes time for me to learn new things.*
>
> **Why does it take time for me to learn new things?**
>
> - I'm not capable of doing anything well.

From this perspective, you have arrived at a different understanding: you realize that, throughout your life, you have withdrawn from things that may have challenged you. You may have conditioned yourself to be someone incapable of learning new talents, doing joyful things, practicing music or playing sports. You have hidden your initial persona whom you feared was not capable of doing anything well.

Next step is to find your worst-case scenario. Ask yourself what the worst-case scenario would be. For example, if you tried to learn new things and couldn't do them well, you would look like you are not good enough. Your initial persona would be exposed. You would feel vulnerable.

Now, you have a new perspective on how you see yourself and how you perceive life. You may be blaming others for taking your personal time away, but also you are not making any effort to establish a new personal routine for yourself, because you don't trust that you are good enough to do anything. You want to keep hiding your vulnerability. Therefore, instead of challenging yourself to get out of your comfort zone and pick up new joyful activities, you settle within your routine and continue doing the things that you are comfortable with.

After arriving at this totally different understanding, reflect on when you may have picked up this underlying fear of not being good enough. Maybe your dad had a competitive spirit and pushed you hard, so that every time you failed to achieve something, he commented on how disappointed he was and how he expected more from you. Maybe your mom was a perfectionist and found mistakes in everything you did. Even though they are not around you now or in control of your life anymore, you have their voices in your head, preventing you from connecting with joyful activities. You fear that you will not be good enough or miserably fail if you take on new activities. As a result of this life conditioning, you procrastinate in attempting to do anything joyful and keep blaming others for not giving you enough time to do so.

While answering these "why" questions to identify your underlying fears and acquire a deeper understanding of your life conditioning, be careful not to point fingers at people, situations and circumstances. This is your internal investigation to access to your own underlying fears and life conditioning. So whenever you find yourself answering a "why" question by focusing on others, immediately turn your attention inward and connect with your own thought patterns and belief systems.

Deepening your Understanding

Once you identify your underlying fears and notice their influence on your life today, you are ready to analyze your past thoroughly. So, start reviewing your family structure and how you grew up. Evaluate your school years and analyze the events you experienced. Examine the interactions you had with family members, friends, peers and schoolmates. In order to do this life review and get a different perspective on your past, talk to your parents, talk to other family members who helped raise you, look at family albums, observe yourself in different life experiences. Connect with those years and find out how happy or sad you were back then.

Following are some sample questions that may help you with your life review to understand some of the specifics of your life conditioning and get to know your initial persona and its antagonist, your conditioned self at a deeper level.

- How was the relationship between your parents?
- What is their view of life?
- What is their life story?
- What is their lifestyle?
- How did they treat you?
- What was your upbringing like?
- What were your family dynamics between you and your parents, and you and your siblings?
- What kind of thoughts and beliefs were imposed on you by your parents, siblings, friends, teachers?
- What were your parents' expectations of you?
- How did your teachers treat you?
- How was your interaction with your friends or classmates?
- What did you think about your life growing up?

During this review, try to understand your life experiences as they relate to you, not how others made you feel or why others treated you the way they did. Just focus on how you felt and thought about a situation, about a trigger event. Each and every life experience is very important. They are part of your make-up and your life conditioning. Discover who your initial persona is and how you developed your conditioned self. Understand what your life has been about. Recognize what made you who you are today.

Note that taking a deeper look at your life and understanding your life conditioning is not an easy task. But, if you'd like to peel off the layers of your life conditioning, the process of understanding is necessary. Opening old wounds is painful. Feeling regret is not pleasant. Facing the guilt and resentment is not comfortable. In addition, gaining a deeper understanding of your life will naturally bring up some anger and sadness that you have repressed throughout your life. In order to progress further in your journey, you need to know how to deal with this repressed anger and sadness.

Dealing with Negative Emotions

Anger

Becoming self-aware and understanding your life conditioning will naturally get you in touch with the repressed anger that you may have felt towards your parents or to those who played a central role in your traumatic life experiences. You may have never had a chance to truly express your initial thoughts and emotions to those who may have mistreated you. Instead, you felt vulnerable and formed your underlying fears. You couldn't dare to tell them how they made you feel. The fire of anger and resentment has kept burning within you and you didn't know how to deal with it. You kept it suppressed.

Similar to the self-awareness process that you studied in the first phase, the practice is to look within and understand your emotions. The attention needs be directed inward. Blaming others for the situations and thinking that *they* made you repress your thoughts and emotions is very natural. You will progress further in your journey when you start to understand your life conditioning better. You will get in touch with how you interpreted your parents' or others' actions and how these perceptions caused you to feel vulnerable.

To deepen this understanding, depending on your own circumstances, it may be a good idea to talk to your parents and other people who emotionally affected you. If you do, you may notice that they don't quite understand where you are coming from. They may have a totally different perspective on what happened. In most cases, in their eyes, they haven't done anything to intentionally hurt you. Keep this point in mind, while confronting them and also while working on releasing your repressed anger.

Let's say you have feared all your life that people will ignore you. As you reach this conclusion through your internal investigation process, you may realize that, deep down, you are angry with your parents for disregarding you. You felt vulnerable and unsafe, as you perceived their treatment as lack of love. You might have thought, "Well, if they loved me enough, they would have paid more attention to me, instead of ignoring me."

Now that you have started digging deeper into the meaning

of your life experiences, you are going to connect with this anger that has been repressed for years. At times, you will notice a force of anger rising up uncontrollably when a situation or person pushes your buttons. Be aware of this anger. You need to stay with this anger. It is very natural to feel this way. It automatically comes out. You can't avoid it. However, you need to be able to deal with it effectively.

Managing this repressed anger will be very difficult in the beginning. Realize that this anger comes from your past. Even though you may project your anger onto others who are in your life today, understand that it is your past that is generating this anger. Notice how people around you make you feel like a victim and powerless again, exactly the way you felt back then. As part of your journey, you need to acknowledge this anger and learn to handle the outburst of this repressed emotion. When observed and managed, anger is a vital part of the healing process. Treat it as a natural step in your journey. Don't force yourself to let it go. Trying to let go will repress your anger even more. Stay with it.

While staying with anger, you may want to use some of the following effective methods that will help you process this intense emotion: At times, you may feel like screaming. Allow yourself to freely scream out loud, wherever possible, in your car, in your living room, in your bathroom—hopefully when nobody is around. While screaming, imagine that with each scream the energy of anger is flowing out of your body. You can also engage in some exercises to move your body to cultivate a better energy flow. While staying with your anger, punch a pillow, attend a kickboxing class, kick a sandbag, walk briskly in a park or spend time in nature.

As you move your body, imagine that the energy of repressed

anger is flowing out of your body. While working on your anger, do some self-reflection. When some deeper insights on your past emerge, write them down in your journal. It is very important to capture the insightful self-knowledge you start to get in touch with.

In addition to these effective methods, refer to the first part of the Rejuvenating your Energy key practice described at the end of this phase for the energetic release of anger.

Sadness

When you deepen your understanding of your life conditioning, you may also experience sadness. As you dig deeper into the meaning of your past, you may start to ask yourself "Why did this have to happen to me?" You may start to feel sad about how you were raised or how you were mistreated or how you didn't do what you wanted or how you missed this or that opportunity due to your underlying fears.

Bringing your attention to your life today, you may still hold your parents or other people responsible for being in this vulnerable position. You feel sad that you are still dealing with the same underlying fears that you had in your childhood. You wish your initial persona weren't vulnerable as you feel now. Whatever the situation was then and it is today, you still have your underlying fears and feel vulnerable.

But now, something is different. You are ready to deal with your past, understand your life and move on. It's true that you can't change anything from the past. But, instead of spending time and energy on what could, should, or would have happened or how things might have been different if you did this or that, how about bringing yourself back to the present and acknowledging that you are here and now.

Understand that your past has made you who you are today. If you are not happy about some aspects of who you are currently, then focus on getting rid of the layers of your life conditioning, release your energy blockages and change your energy level to break your life patterns. Make a firmer commitment to work on your conditioned self and get ready to take actions and make conscious efforts that will allow your authentic self to emerge in your life—today, tomorrow and every day for the rest of your life.

Embrace the idea that you can only move forward from here. Understanding your past and naturally grieving about what happened will make you stronger for the rest of your journey. So stay with sadness. Observe your sadness. Understand your sadness. Recognizing your underlying fears and understanding your life conditioning is starting to help you get to some concrete answers as to why you keep living your limiting life patterns. The life conditioning that has held you back throughout your life is about to lose its power over you.

While staying with sadness, apply some of the following methods that will help you effectively process it. First of all, do not hold your tears. Cry. Tears are a form of release. So cry freely, without holding anything back. Take long walks in nature and connect with the beauty surrounding you and breathe in the fresh air. When a deeper understanding of your life conditioning surfaces, write it down in your journal.

In addition to these effective methods, refer to the first part of the Rejuvenating your Energy key practice described at the end of this phase to energetically release sadness and related energy blockages.

Key Energy: Self-Compassion

Becoming aware of your conditioned self, your underlying fears and understanding your life conditioning are not easy to do. As part of your journey, you have to face the emotional pain and suffering that you have had in your life. Allow yourself open up to all the uncomfortable memories that you have wanted to suppress for a long time. You may have never wanted to think about them again. Embrace your past as well as your life today the way it is. You now have access to the system of life. You now know that life flows in a certain way so that you can cleanse all of those repressed emotions from your past and get rid of your life conditioning so that you can and will achieve your highest potential.

During your review of what happened in your past, you may encounter some inner thoughts of which you were not aware. You may realize how much you judge yourself. You may also get in touch with your initial persona's self-image of being a failure, not important, inadequate or not lovable. In reality, most of these feelings, along with self-blame and self-criticism are part of your thought patterns and belief systems that feed your underlying fears. Notice and acknowledge these thoughts and beliefs that you run in your mind and let them come out into your conscious.

Understanding your life conditioning reveals all of those thoughts and beliefs that you have been holding about yourself. It also allows you to come to terms with your self-judgment and what really happened in your life. Connect with your heart and embrace your past as it is. Acknowledge what happened and how you feel about it. Instead of judging and blaming yourself again, objectively review some of the memories of incidents or events that formed your negative thought patterns and belief systems.

Staying at a distance and witnessing yourself in these situations will make you realize that the way you have behaved and responded to each particular situation might have been the only option available to you at that time. Most probably, anybody in your shoes who experienced the same situations would have reacted in a similar way. You have done your best to cope with these situations. See things through your heart. Be understanding, accepting, tolerant and gentle with yourself. Realize that what you have experienced in your past is your guidance to get to know your conditioned self and initial persona. The self-knowledge you acquire from your past experiences becomes a vehicle to a better future. You are on your way towards your highest potential.

Key Practice: Rejuvenating your Energy

Energy rejuvenation means recycling the stagnant energy that has a low vibration with a new, powerful energy that vibrates at a higher frequency. In order to rejuvenate your energy, you first need to get rid of the low energy of negative emotions. In the second part of the energetic rejuvenation process, you cultivate your energy by tapping into a strong energy resource.

First, let's release the stagnant energy.

I. Releasing Negative Emotions

Emotions are energy. In order to release a negative emotion, you need to connect with its energy by locating it in your body. In order to spot the energy of a negative emotion, you need to perform a body scan as follows:

Sit comfortable, your mind calm and your body fully relaxed. Close your eyes and start scanning your body using your mind's eye. Just go through your body systematically, part by part, from head to toe. Observe each part of your body and notice if there is any tension or tightness in the area. If so, stay with this uncomfortable sensation and see whether you can associate it with any negative emotion. You can bring your awareness to the area of tension or energetic congestion and find out what you are holding there.

For example, sometimes anger may show up as tension in your shoulders or neck. Sometimes, sadness may appear in the center of your chest. Sometimes, your anxiety may show up in your stomach. Just calmly observe what's going on in your body. Simply connect with any negative emotion that your body is holding in.

For some reason, if you can't notice any tense or uncomfortable area in your body associated with anger, sadness or other negative emotions, just hold the energy of the specific emotion in front of your body and observe it from a distance. Without intensely feeling it, capture and acknowledge the energy of that emotion.

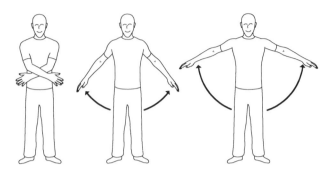

Illustration 8. Releasing Negative Emotions

Now you are ready to energetically release your negative emotions. Stand up with your feet shoulder width apart. Eyes are open. Slightly cross your arms in front of you at your belly button level. Connect with the area of your body that holds the particular negative emotion in or directly connect with the emotion you are holding in front of your body. Now, forcefully swing your arms to your sides and push the energy of anger, sadness or any other negative emotion out of your body through your palms and through your fingertips. Visualize an outflow of the negative emotion in the form of energy.

While swinging your arms to the side, use your breath to push the energy of that negative emotion out of your mouth. Forcefully exhale, as you swing your arms out. Then, gently inhale while softly bringing your arms back towards your body, slightly crossing them in front of your belly button. While pushing the negative emotions out of your body, you may feel tingling sensations on your palms and fingertips. This tingling sensation is the natural effect of the energetic outflow.

Without pausing, forcefully swing your hands out again, your arms following your hands. Every time you swing your arms out, forcefully exhale and imagine the energy of the negative emotion flowing out of your palms and fingertips.

Any time you feel a negative emotion, perform a body scan and repeat this energetic release of your negative emotions for about ten to fifteen times. If you feel dizzy, sit down and relax your body.

II. Replenishing your Energy

After you release your negative emotions, it is important to replenish your energy so that you can raise your energy level. As you know, nature provides great resources that you can use to replenish your energy. You can definitely relate to how relaxing it is to be in nature and how rejuvenated you feel after a beautiful hike among trees. But, if you don't have time to go to nature often enough, would you like to connect with nature's energy at home or in your neighborhood?

The best resources for replenishing your energy are evergreen trees like pines, willows, redwoods and cypresses. Look for one of these trees in your neighborhood or nearby parks. For your home or for your office, the best resource is water bamboo. They have great energy. Be it a pine tree in the neighborhood or a water bamboo at your home or on your desk at work, all you need to do is stand next to it, with palms facing towards the evergreen tree or the water bamboo (the "plant").

Illustration 9. Replenishing Your Energy

The *center* of your palms should face the plant. Focus on your palms. When your energy interacts with the plant's energy, you may feel a gentle pull. This means that new energy is flowing from the plant through your palms into your body. Due to this energy flow, you may also feel some tingling in your palms. Try it. Do you feel the energy flow into your body, within your body?

In terms of practice time, five to seven minutes, once or twice a week will be enough to replenish your energy. Do it whenever your body and mind need such energetic replenishment. You can practice this technique for a few minutes each time after you energetically release your negative emotions. The best practice time is during the day, especially in the mornings, when nature's energy is fresh and strong.

5 · Expanding Your Boundaries

SO FAR ON YOUR JOURNEY, you have been observing the actions of your conditioned self and reviewing your current and past life experiences to deepen the understanding of your life conditioning. Now, you are about to enter an important phase where you will be asked to take actions to override your conditioned self so that you can expand your boundaries.

You always defend your conditioned self and hide your vulnerability because you perceive every trigger event as an attack to your conditioned self. Therefore, it's not going to be easy to override your conditioned self and expose your vulnerability. However, on the other hand, your defensive actions come with some consequences. First, you exert a lot of energy. Second, to effectively protect your conditioned self from future trigger events, you contract your boundaries and withdraw yourself into your comfort zone. Understandably, you stay behind those tightly contracted boundaries and refrain yourself from taking any actions that may further expose your vulnerability. So you keep hiding behind the mask of your conditioned self and go on with your daily routine, staying on the same energy level.

How can you break your limiting life patterns, when you stay on that same energy level and within the same contracted boundaries where you were afraid to express your thoughts and emotions and formed your energy blockages in the first place? You need to do something different to raise your energy level. Since your standard, conditioned defense mechanisms do not only repress your initial thoughts and emotions, but further drain your energy, you need to change the way you defend your conditioned self.

Before you learn about the actions that you can consciously take to override your conditioned self, expand your boundaries and raise your energy level, let's understand what your defense mechanisms are and observe how you use them to protect your conditioned self.

Defense Mechanisms

Imagine that another trigger event provokes you. Your perceptions immediately tell you that you are under attack. Your conditioned self feels threatened. You take the situation personally. You react to it emotionally and automatically launch your defense mechanisms, which are merely your unconscious—energetically conditioned—efforts to protect your conditioned self's image and hide your vulnerability.

Defense mechanisms can be short-term and long-term.

I. Short-term Defense Mechanisms

The short-term defense mechanisms are the strategies that are designed to ward off the immediate threat that a trigger event poses to your conditioned self. These strategies can be categorized as aggressive, passive-aggressive and passive.

Aggressive Strategies

You may launch your aggressive strategies, when you want to handle the threat you are facing with force. In some situations, you may feel that a lot of things are at stake. You may find yourself yelling, cursing, blaming or overpowering. Whenever you face particular trigger events, you feel the need to aggressively protect your conditioned self's image. The intensity of your aggressive actions is directly proportional to how vulnerable situations or people make you feel.

The other component of an aggressive strategy is to exert some level of authority or power over a situation or person. You feel that you can afford to use an aggressive tone and style to defend your conditioned self and hide your vulnerability. Your aggressive actions show everyone that you are upset and have the power to change things around. Your motive is to immediately control the situation or the people so that you defuse the threat and feel safer.

Passive-Aggressive Strategies

You may use your passive-aggressive strategies, when you want to ward off the threat or perceived personal attack, but don't feel powerful enough to do it directly and aggressively. As a result, you choose indirect ways to defend your conditioned self. Some of the actions you take may include sarcasm, gossiping, labeling, or judging. Your motive is to deflect the hurt and discomfort the trigger event has caused. Your passive-aggressive strategies make you feel that you have gotten even with the person who triggered you, and therefore, you now feel relieved and safer.

You may resort to your passive strategies when you feel absolutely powerless against the situation or the people that challenge you and impose a threat to your conditioned self. In these circumstances, you feel very vulnerable and therefore may want to run away from the situation or the person, so that you can protect yourself from the source of emotional pain and discomfort. Your goal is to build a very thick and tall wall around you to completely isolate yourself and withdraw from everything. You feel safer behind those walls.

II. Long-term Defense Mechanisms

Whenever you feel under attack, you launch one of the above short-term defense mechanisms. You will temporarily feel safer. However, these strategies do not eliminate your vulnerability completely. You realize that you keep launching these defense mechanisms and nothing changes. You still feel vulnerable. Feeling stuck and trapped in your vulnerability, you feel powerless. Your emotional pain and suffering continue.

To cope with this emotional pain and suffering, you launch your long-term defense mechanisms, which are your addictive behaviors. In order to avoid a face-to-face encounter with a trigger event, you choose to numb your vulnerability behind the comfort you receive from external resources such as food, alcohol, smoking, sex, gambling, overworking or keeping yourself busy.

Like the short-term defense mechanisms, your actions under the long-term defense mechanisms will provide you with some temporary relief from your emotional pain and suffering. You will feel safer for a brief moment, until you face the next trigger event, and confront your underlying fear and feel vulnerable—again. You soon realize that your defense mechanisms drain your energy in the long run and those "happy" and "safe" moments fade away quickly.

You feel that your efforts to escape from your current situation have been in vain. You realize that you can't run away from the vulnerability of your initial persona. You are back—again—where you started. You feel exhausted and defeated. Nothing changes in your life. As a result, you feel more vulnerable and powerless and contract your boundaries even more. Now, they are so tight and narrow, there is not much room for your authentic self to emerge.

Facing your Underlying Fears

Throughout your life, in order to survive and fit in—and disguise your initial persona, you have been exerting a lot of energy. When you are in that kind of survival mode, you contract your boundaries and mostly conform to others' rules and expectations. You refrain from fully exploring life. You get into a routine that you are comfortable with and withdraw into your contracted boundaries. As a result, you hold your true essence back so that you can securely maintain the mask of your conditioned self to hide the vulnerability of your initial persona and feel safe.

This conformity is the main reason why you are not living as your authentic self right now. Behind the mask of your conditioned self, you feel vulnerable all the time and afraid to take steps to allow your authentic self to show up. You feel low, anxious, depressed, withdrawn, easily agitated and indecisive whenever you anticipate a threat. At that low energy level, you don't know what to do or where to go. Staying within your contracted boundaries, you feel boxed in, trapped and suffocated most of the time. You need to expand those boundaries to liberate your true essence.

You can only eliminate your vulnerability, if you are willing to face your underlying fears. Going against your fears means *doing the opposite* of what your conditioned self has been doing. This duel between your conditioned self and the underlying fears of your initial persona that you have been trying to escape from is a challenging one—but, something you need to go through. If you can eliminate your vulnerability by overcoming your underlying fears, there won't be a need to defend your conditioned self and launch any of your defense mechanisms. You can only win this duel, if you are ready and willing to override the initial instructions that you gave your conditioned self.

Overriding your conditioned self means courageously exposing your vulnerability by doing just the opposite of what your conditioned self is programmed to do.

Doing the Opposite

If you want to expand your boundaries, you need to face your underlying fears, which requires stepping out of your comfort zone and acting against your conditioned self. Since what you have been doing so far has contracted your boundaries and drained your energy, you will need to do the opposite of what you have been doing. Only then can you push your boundaries out and overcome the vulnerability of your initial persona.

When you feel the urge to revert back to your defense mechanisms, *doing the opposite* or something different other than your typical defense mechanism is a very scary proposition. A particular defense mechanism you want to override has been your go-to action. It gave you a sense of comfort and safety. *Doing the opposite* may feel like jumping off the cliff—not literally of course, but as a feeling—where you feel that you are doing something totally against your nature. Do not worry! When you start taking actions different from your defense mechanisms, the increase in your energy level will lift you up.

Following are some actions that you can consciously choose to take in order to expand your boundaries and challenge your conditioned self. Note that the conditioned self suggested below is only one of the possible identities you may have assumed to hide your vulnerability and disguise your initial persona. Until now, your initial persona has been hiding behind the mask of your conditioned self. Now, can you dare to unmask your conditioned self and face your vulnerability and your underlying fears?

Let's examine *doing the opposite* in the context of common fears.

Fear of Not Being Good Enough

Underlying Fear: You fear that you are not good enough.

Conditioned self: You may be a perfectionist. You may want to excel in everything you do until you exhaust yourself. Since you want to be the best, you may have become a workaholic. You may have a controlling personality with a strong need to feel everything is under your control.

Doing the Opposite: Instead of trying to be perfect and double checking everything, can you allow yourself to make mistakes—just for once? In your relationship, when you want things to be under control, instead of trying to fix everything and change your partner, can you just ignore your partner's messiness or tardiness for a while? In order to feel safe, you constantly try to prove that you are good enough. Can you allow yourself to enjoy an activity, instead of trying to master it like a task?

Fear of Abandonment

Underlying Fear: You fear that people will abandon you one day or turn their back on you unexpectedly.

Conditioned self: You may withdraw from people, choose not to trust them, or take a long time to establish deep connections with people. You may have an introverted personality.

Doing the Opposite: If you have a partner who is emotionally unavailable or noncommittal about the future of your relationship, can you stop checking in regularly to find out what they are up to? Instead, can you focus on what you need to attend in your own life? In order to feel safe, you constantly expect your partner to do something to prove their love to you. Instead, can you look at your relationship and identify the things that your partner has already done to show their love to you?

Fear of Failure

Underlying Fear: You fear that you may be a failure and incapable of doing something right or succeeding in anything.

Conditioned self: You may be a procrastinator. You may have difficult time in focusing on what you need to do. Your attention may be easily distracted by other projects that are not important, preventing you from completing your main project. As a result, you avoid or delay facing your vulnerability that you are a failure.

Doing the Opposite: Since you have been doing the self-observation meditation for a while, can you try to focus on one project at a time? Can you identify the resistance? Whenever other things distract you, can you observe that you are afraid of completing your main project? Can you recognize that you are being pulled away, so that you can't finish what you are working on? Alternatively, when you force yourself to do something, can you relax and not think about the outcome? Just take it out of your to-do-list and regularly attend your project because you want to.

Fear of Rejection

Underlying Fear: You fear that you may not be worthy of being loved.

Conditioned self: You may be a people pleaser. You want to accommodate people around you and place their needs above your own.

Doing the Opposite: Whenever you feel that your "people pleaser" conditioning is being taken advantage of, how can you claim your self-worth? For example, can you stop being the designated driver for once when you go out with friends? Instead, can you let them take a cab home? Instead of listening to your friend talk about their problems for hours without any concern for your issues, can you gently tell your friend that you also have a few problems that you are dealing with and that you'd like to get their opinion on?

Fear of Loneliness

Underlying Fear: You fear that you may be lonely for the rest of your life.

Conditioned self: You may be a social butterfly. You may be someone very easy to talk to and connect with.

Doing the Opposite: Can you stay at home on a Friday night, instead of going out with your friends? Can you cut down on social events and focus on what you'd like to do by yourself in your free time? Instead of having too many friends, can you invest more time and effort into one or two relationships where you feel a deeper connection?

Dealing with Common Challenges

Have you figured out the actions that you want to take to remove the mask of your conditioned self? You sense it already. Taking actions to override your conditioned self and face your underlying fears is extremely difficult. You are stepping out of your comfort zone and entering into unchartered territories. Following the *doing the opposite* exercises will be nerve wracking. Again, it will feel like you are being asked to jump off a cliff. Every seeker on the path to his or her highest potential has to go through this step. So be gentle with yourself. After taking a few conscious steps, you will start to expand your boundaries. Initially, you couldn't dare to jump, but now that you have, *doing the opposite* will feel very exhilarating—it will feel like you are flying... like you are free.

Simply Saying No

To simplify the process of *doing the opposite*, let's review another strategy that will help you unmask your conditioned self. The strategy is simply saying *no* to the things you have been saying, *yes* to, and vice versa. If you have withdrawn yourself behind your contracted boundaries and been saying *no* to things, it's time to say *yes* to the opportunities that are in front of you. Alternatively, if you feel like you don't have any personal time for yourself because you have given it away to accommodate others, start saying *no* to some of the things that are not important or not urgent.

While going through the things you want to say *yes* to, identify the activities that are joyful and nurturing to your mind and body. You have created your conditioned self to hide your vulnerability, so your default choice is always to stay within your comfort zone. Due to this choice, you have stayed in your routine and allocated very little time to yourself. *Doing the opposite* can also mean incorporating new joyful activities that nurture your mind, body and soul—something that you may have not done before. Whenever you notice that you are stuck and bored, ask yourself "What would be a fun thing to do right now?" Follow through your reply by saying *yes* to something that lifts your spirits and brings joy into your life.

One out of One Hundred Rule

When expanding your boundaries, the stakes are high. Therefore, don't expect to start doing the opposite right away. Expect some transition time. In the beginning, let's keep the bar as low as possible. Let's have a simple rule. Can you aim to take an opposite action only once out of hundred opportunities?

Even with this one-out-of-hundred rule, it is very difficult to override your conditioned self and break the energetic wiring. Keep your composure and stay alert. Even if you failed to do the opposite for hundreds of times, forget all about the previous chances that you have blown away and just focus on the next opportunity. Be patient with yourself. Expanding boundaries takes time.

Dealing with Guilt

While expanding your boundaries, you will take conscious steps that you haven't taken until now. These out-of-routine actions will make you feel uncomfortable, strange and even guilty. You will feel like you are abandoning your conditioned self. The voice in your head may tell you that you should stay within your contracted boundaries and keep hiding your initial persona. Your inner voice may want you to keep the status quo, no matter how unbearable it may feel at times. That inner voice is the voice of your conditioned self.

Throughout your life, you have been acting to protect your vulnerability. You can't change everything overnight. Going against how you are energetically wired will make you feel that you are betraying your conditioned self and your initial persona. When you choose to do a joyful and nurturing activity, you may feel that you are not supposed to have fun. You may feel guilty for doing things for yourself. Just recognize this guilt. Understand where it comes from. Discover the underlying fears, thought patterns and belief systems that feed this intense emotion—and *do the opposite* anyway.

Key Energy: Courage

Throughout life, unless you've been under extreme danger or had enough of some trying situations, you have rarely ventured beyond the identity of your conditioned self. The reason for keeping your boundaries as contracted as they are today is that you haven't had enough courage to overcome your underlying fears.

You need the energy of courage to take steps to expand your boundaries so that you can increase your energy level. In order to connect with courage, you must keep taking conscious steps to overcome your underlying fears. Apply the *one-out-of-hundred* rule, and look for the next opportunity, instead of grieving over the last ninety-nine opportunities you may have missed. Stay mindful of those moments where you can consciously choose your next actions to override your defense mechanisms and unmask your conditioned self.

After taking such courageous steps, you will feel exhilarated and empowered. In those moments, though rare in the beginning of your journey but abundantly available to you in later phases, you feel totally connected to everything around you. You will begin to see other choices of action and different routes available to you that were not visible before.

Remember, there is only one person who determines the limits of your boundaries, and that's you. Nobody else.

Key Practice: Expanding your Energy

The following key practice will help you energetically expand your boundaries from within. As a result, you will be able to connect with the energy of courage. This energetic expansion meditation requires a constant concentration on the center of your body, which is about three finger widths below your belly button. This point is called the life force energy center. By keeping your focus on this energy center, you will be able to cultivate your energy and feel a subtle expansion in your energy body.

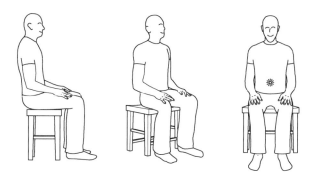

Illustration 10. Energetic Expansion Meditation

You can start practicing this meditation technique for five minutes, right after you finish your self-observation meditation practice in the mornings. To transition to energetic expansion meditation, you will only need to change your hand positions while maintaining the same sitting posture. Also, your focus will shift onto your life force energy center, instead of your thumbs.

If you prefer to practice this technique separately, instead of practicing it after self-observation meditation, then first, find a comfortable place to sit. Then, place your feet flat on the floor at shoulder width apart. Your knees are at a ninety-degree angle. Your back is in upright position, straight but not stiff. Your shoulders, neck and head are all relaxed.

Place your hands on your thighs, palms facing down. With palms resting on your thighs, keep your arms relaxed. Elbows can be bent to keep your arms fairly relaxed and free of tension. Take a deep breath in, and when exhaling close your eyes. Place your tongue gently on the roof of your mouth and put the tip of your tongue behind your front teeth. Keep your mouth closed, breathing naturally.

Observe your thoughts and images as they pass through your mind. Acknowledge them. Try to stay detached and indifferent to your thoughts. Now, slowly place your concentration on the life force energy center. It may be challenging in the beginning, but try to keep your focus on that point throughout your entire practice. Stay alert. If you are distracted by your thoughts or lose your concentration, bring your attention gently back to the life force energy center.

After focusing on that point for a while, your undivided attention will activate your life force energy, raise your energy level and enhance the flow of energy within your body. As a result, you may sense a subtle expansion of your energy. What you may exactly feel varies from person to person. Some of the more common sensations include tingling, a cold or warm breeze or a subtle moving sensation within the body.

When you sense your energy level increase and your energy body expand, visualize an energetic bubble surrounding your body that continues to expand. This sensation may feel like ripples of energy waves spreading from the center of your body outward to every direction. Imagine that this expanding energy encircles you with a beautiful, protective bubble. You may choose to color the inside and the borders of this bubble that is surrounding you.

Check in with how you feel now. Being in the center of this bubble may feel safe and comfortable. Visualize how the expanded energy forms a safety buffer between you and the outside world. While still observing and witnessing the sensations, keep your focus on the life force energy center. Connect with your energy. Just acknowledge what's going on.

Now, invite a particularly challenging situation to your mind. Gently review the defense mechanism you have used to defend your conditioned self in this situation. What is your perception? Why do you defend your conditioned self? From a distance, witness yourself taking a certain trigger event personally and launching your typical strategy to ward off the perceived attack. Observe your conditioned self and the situation with a certain indifference and detachment.

While witnessing your reaction, do you recognize your underlying fear? What are you protecting your conditioned self from? Do you identify the traits of your conditioned self?

If you feel distracted and lose the sense of indifference and detachment, bring yourself back to the inside of the bubble. Reconnect with the expanded energy that surrounds you.

Now, connect with the energy of courage and imagine an alternative course of action. What do you really feel like doing? How would you like to respond to this trigger event? Challenge yourself and see whether you could face your underlying fears. What is the opposite course of action that you have always wanted to take, but never have?

Visualize raising your hand up or pushing your hands outward to hold the situation or the people outside of the energetic bubble, i.e. your boundaries. When facing similar trigger events in the future, can you imagine simply saying no? Will you be able to put your foot down and respond differently? Can you imagine yourself courageously sharing your thoughts and feelings with others? What other possible actions do you foresee taking?

While going through these scenarios in your head and visualizing the bubble encircling your body, anchor yourself on that energy of courage you have connected with. From now on, whenever you face a trigger event, go back to this energy by visualizing the energetic bubble surrounding your body and helping you expand your boundaries. Connect with courage, stay committed to take conscious actions to override your defense mechanisms of your conditioned self and overcome your underlying fears. Simply acknowledge the boundaries you have created around your body and keep them expanded throughout your day.

To finish your meditation practice, place your hands on top of each other and put them on your life force energy center. Imagine that you are bringing the expanded energy back to its source and putting a lid on top to preserve it. Take three deep breaths in, then exhale slowly and gently.

Open your eyes, bring yourself back to full consciousness. Reflect on how your meditation went. Feeling relaxed, empowered and courageous, do a little stretch for a minute or two to let your physical body feel this new energy.

6 · Building Your Solid Foundation

CONSTANTLY WORKING on expanding your boundaries is difficult. It requires dedicated self-observation practice in every moment of your day. Getting out of your defense mechanisms that you launch to protect your conditioned self will require courage and strong will.

Remember that the self-realization journey is a life long process. Building a solid foundation is a major milestone in your journey. If you haven't had a chance to apply the *doing the opposite* technique yet, your energy level may have not increased enough to notice a positive shift in your life flow. If so, I highly recommend you to re-study the previous three phases and try again to courageously take actions to override your conditioned self and overcome your underlying fears before you continue with this next phase of your journey.

Consider the steps you are taking as part of a process. You don't need to rush. Do little things that are different and not part of the identity of your conditioned self. Taking courageous actions to expand your boundaries has already started to increase your energy level. Due to this expansion, you may also notice the difference in how you respond to trigger events these days. In order to maintain your newly expanded boundaries and also be able to take even more steps to increase your energy level further, you need to have a solid foundation that supports your actions. The more solid your foundation, the more mindful and confident your actions will be.

Like the work you have done so far, you will build your solid foundation step by step. View this foundation as your platform from where you will be launching the remaining phases of your journey toward achieving your highest potential. By now, hopefully, you have done enough work to get to know your conditioned self and your initial persona. You now have a better understanding of your life conditioning. Consider every little step you have taken so far, every little insight you have gained through self-observation, as bricks that you will use to build a solid foundation.

In order to build your solid foundation, you need to learn how to ground yourself, center your emotions and balance your actions. Let's examine each of these steps thoroughly.

Grounding

Grounding means to hold your expanded boundaries intact while facing a trigger event so that you can short circuit the impact of a perceived attack and observe your initial thought patterns and belief systems that feed your perceptions.

In order to ground your energy, you need to connect with the earth's energy. This connection will help you hold your expanded boundaries intact. When you feel grounded and energetically stronger, you will be able to face a trigger event without immediately launching your defense mechanisms. As a result, you will be able to preserve your energy and stay grounded for longer periods of time. Whenever a trigger event causes you to feel vulnerable, think about the bottoms of your feet and feel the ground you are standing on. You will immediately connect with the earth's energy and feel grounded.

The goal of grounding is to defuse the trigger event and not to be consumed by it. The issue is that the time that lapses between a trigger event and your emotional reaction is too short. By the time you realize that you are dealing with a trigger event, you will find yourself already overwhelmed by intense emotional reactions and launching your defense mechanisms. At that moment, your efforts to defend your conditioned self drain your energy.

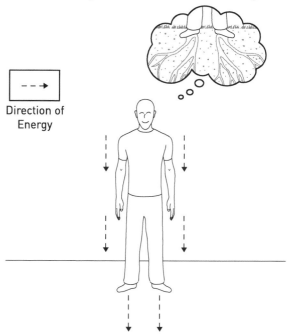

Illustration 11. Grounding

The earth's energy is very powerful. When you connect with it through the bottoms of your feet, you feel the strength that flows from the earth into your body. Through this connection, you feel like you're standing on a strong platform that is holding you safely. You feel supported and are now able to ward off perceived threats to your conditioned self.

This grounding practice helps you create the necessary time gap between a trigger event and your intense emotional reaction. At that exact moment, you will be able to step back from the situation, and have the opportunity to observe the thought patterns and belief systems, that make you believe that you are under attack. Now, you are digging deeply into your perceptions. During the time gap you created through grounding, observe how you have perceived the trigger event. Notice your thoughts and beliefs about the situation or the person confronting you. Understand why you are taking the triggers—someone's actions, attitudes, statements or facial expressions—personally.

Let's say you have fear of rejection that creates social anxiety whenever you have to speak in front of a group. You always get nervous before these presentations because your confident and self-assured conditioned self seems to be threatened by the possible rejection from the people in the meeting.

Whenever you detect a trigger event provoking your intense emotional reactions, you need to ground yourself through the bottoms of your feet. Let's say you are about to go into a meeting and make a presentation to the management team. You are anxious and nervous. Can you separate yourself from the situation by focusing on the bottoms of your feet? Now, observe your thought patterns and belief systems that feed your anxiety and the nervousness.

You know how to expand your boundaries. So let's review some of your options in this situation. After grounding yourself through the bottoms of your feet, allow yourself to *do the opposite* of what you would have done in the past. For example, can you be just yourself at the meeting, instead of your conditioned self who wants to prove itself? Do you really feel you need to impress everyone? While presenting, can you stop reading people's facial expressions to find out whether your presentation is going well or not? Can you allow yourself to be nervous and anxious, understanding your initial persona's vulnerability?

Only when you ground yourself and take a step back from the situation will a different alternative course of actions appear in front of you. Choose consciously.

Centering

Centering means, while grounded, to direct your attention inward so that you can calm your emotions by observing your intense emotional reactions.

Once your connection to the earth's energy is established, you are ready to center yourself. Centering is a practice of deeper self-observation to calm your emotions. In order to put this into action, whenever you feel the intense emotional reaction bubbling up within you, immediately turn your attention to your breath. The way you are breathing is a great indicator of how vulnerable your conditioned self feels at that moment. When you feel very vulnerable and under attack, your breathing tends to be very shallow. Observe your breath and notice your state of mind.

In response to a trigger event, let's say that you have taken a course of action, either your typical defense mechanism or your *doing the opposite* action that will expand your boundaries. Whatever you do, you will end up dealing with a lot of emotions. Not knowing how to handle all these intense emotions, you may enter into a period of confusion and conflict. You may get into arguments with your loved ones, you may decide to look for another job or you may choose not to call your friend for a while. These events may overwhelm you. But, at the same time, they provide a perfect opportunity to center yourself. Simply bring your attention to your breath for a few seconds and then, observe your intense emotional reactions.

Let's say your conditioned self is a people pleaser. Your underlying fear is fear of rejection and your vulnerability is that you feel worthless. Suppose one of your friends asked you to drop them off to the airport that afternoon. Even though you had a few meetings and errands planned, you immediately said yes—even though you felt resentment inside. Nonetheless, you drove to your friend's house to pick them up. As usual, they were late to come down. And then, all the way to the airport, your friend complained about everything in their life. At the end, all you got was just a plain thank you, as if it was your duty to give them a ride.

In this hypothetical scenario, you went along with your defense mechanisms. In other words, as your conditioned self, you went out of your way to accommodate your friend. How do you feel? Maybe, you are little upset with your friend that they weren't as appreciative as you expected them to be, or maybe, you are angry with them that they didn't care about your problems, and only talked about theirs, or maybe you are angry at yourself that you went out of your way and cancelled your plans—again!—for a friend, who didn't recognize your efforts and what you did for them. Your friend always calls you when they need something from you, but they are never available when you need something from them. You feel used and manipulated. Your intense emotions of anger, frustration and sadness start to overwhelm you. It's time to center yourself.

Let's say you decided to expand your boundaries and tried to do something different. For example, when your friend called you again, you told them that you were busy and couldn't take them to the airport because you had some errands to do that afternoon. You may feel okay for a while, but then not taking your friend to the airport will make you feel guilty and uncomfortable. Questions like what if they think you are selfish or what if they never talk to you again will start to run through your mind. Your *doing the opposite* action will poke at your underlying fears of rejection and make you uncomfortable and anxious along with guilt that you didn't accommodate your friend's request.

While expanding your boundaries, you will find yourself at this crossroad over and over again. Should you continue with the actions of your conditioned self or should you try to do something different? You may try out various alternative actions in different circumstances. Be creative. Be spontaneous. More importantly center yourself before you take any actions.

Trying to decide between different alternatives, acting like your conditioned self or doing something against your conditioned self may be emotionally overwhelming in the beginning. You will be experiencing your old emotions when you feel under attack from a trigger event and new emotions when you unmask your conditioned self. For example, anger could be an old emotion you felt when others did not appreciate your efforts when you put their needs above yours. When you decide to do the opposite and allocate more time to the things that you enjoy, then guilt might be your new emotion.

Whenever you feel an intense emotion remember to immediately bring your attention to your breath and center yourself.

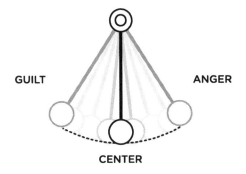

Illustration 12. Pendulum

Like a pendulum finding its center, you will eventually find your center between these overwhelming emotions. Keep taking actions and stay with the arising emotions. They are neither good nor bad. You feel them because of your life conditioning. In each and every situation, through inward attention, you will gain a deeper understanding of how your thoughts patterns and belief systems affect your emotions. You will soon notice that your intense emotions start to slowly calm down. You are centering yourself.

Balancing

Balancing means, while grounded and centered, to consciously adjust your actions.

In the past, with almost no boundaries in place and no solid foundation to stand on, whenever you lost your ground and got off-center, you immediately felt more vulnerable. As your conditioned response, you attacked back and lost your center even more. So without grounding and centering, you were completely off balance. Your emotions were all over the place. Your defense mechanisms kept draining your energy.

At this point, you know how to maintain your expanded boundaries through grounding and centering. It's time to learn to find balance in your actions to complete the construction of your solid foundation. The importance of balancing is to be able to adjust your actions after you calm your emotions.

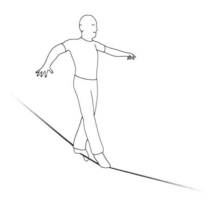

Illustration 13. Tightrope Walker

In order to understand the concept of balance, let's take a look at a tightrope walker. They may appear to have, or be in, perfect balance. Yet, observing more closely, you will find out that what you perceive as balance is really an act of constant balancing. As a matter of fact, you will notice the tightrope walker continually takes a series of actions—small adjustments and corrections—to maintain their balance. The system of life requires exactly these types of adjustments and corrections to your daily routine and to your actions, so that you can bring a sustainable change to your life.

Now look back at your *doing the opposite* action of not taking your friend to the airport. You have expanded your boundaries. Now, let's find balance. When your friend calls you next time, what will your response be? Maybe, you will choose to go out of your way and give them a lift to the airport. But this time, can you calm your emotions and adjust your actions? For example, while you're driving your friend to the airport, can you gently mention that you are upset that they only call you when they need something from you? Notice the adjustment in your actions. Observe how much, through these new conscious actions, you will still feel vulnerable. Acknowledge your underlying fears. You are in the process of unmasking your conditioned self. Only through these small adjustments will you be able to find your balance and stand on your solid foundation to alter your reactions to trigger events.

While trying to find balance, you may realize that this process is a constant back and forth. Not having an immediate tangible progress may upset you. Don't give in to your disappointment. It's okay if you can't override your conditioned self's actions immediately. But, understand that it's always *your choice* to adjust your actions. Practice self-observation, conduct your internal investigation and work on building a solid foundation. Explore what you can do differently. Whether you feel vulnerable and need to protect your conditioned self, or you do the opposite and face your vulnerability, keep grounding, centering and balancing whatever the situation is. Only through these small adjustments and corrections, which are integral part of your journey, can you stay on course to meet your authentic self and achieve your highest potential. You are closer than you think.

Grounding instead of Letting Go

Whenever you face a challenging life situation or difficult people, you often hear the advice to "just let it go." When your buttons are being pushed, there is no simple technique for letting go. You can't easily drop your intense emotions entirely. You can't all of a sudden reverse your emotional reactions in the heat of the moment. A particular action, attitude, comment or gesture makes you feel vulnerable. You feel that you are personally attacked. So, of course, you will take it seriously, respond with an intense emotional reaction and protect your conditioned self.

Throughout your journey within, instead of forcing yourself to let go of your intense emotions, allow your emotions to surface. That's how you can work on overriding your conditioned self. Just be gentle with yourself about how you feel. Recognize your initial persona. Try to understand your life conditioning and identify the related underlying fears as the intense emotions arise within you. Keep practicing self-observation and be present in every moment to build your solid foundation. You will soon realize that grounding, centering and balancing become second nature to you. In the near future, you won't need to let anything go, because the triggers will not be able to poke at you like they did before.

Building Your Solid Foundation at Work

Suppose you are an ambitious and goal oriented person. You always aim to excel in what you do. Let's say you started a new position at a company about six months ago. Naturally, you are very excited about your new role. You already have plans to make a difference in this company.

Right after you start your job, due to your ambitious nature and also to prove yourself, you start to get involved with projects outside the scope of your work to make needed process improvements within the company.

In a sense, you always want to be a good corporate citizen, and jump in and improve everything. Essentially, you have an underlying fear of rejection so you try to do a good job over and above what's required by your job description. You want to feel important and accepted for your efforts.

As you get involved, you start to expect the same quality of work and effectiveness from your colleagues. They don't seem to meet your high expectations. You always pride yourself on paying attention to detail and try to do your best. You feel like you are carrying the whole organization on your shoulders. Nobody else seems to be pulling their weight. All of the extra work you put in makes you feel resentment towards your colleagues.

You are extremely disappointed that others don't attempt to do their best. They don't seem to care. You complain and share your disappointment with your colleagues. Your frustration starts to come out as anger, blame or withdrawal. The more you complain in the company, the more agitated you become.

Your high expectations slowly begin to annoy your coworkers. They start to stay away from you and ignore you and your efforts to make things better.

Sensing this attitude towards you, you start to take things more personally. Every email, every meeting or every conversation starts to frustrate you and poke at your underlying fears of not being recognized. You start to feel more vulnerable as your efforts are not appreciated. Feeling intense anger and frustration, you immediately launch your defense mechanism of blaming others, "They don't understand me!"

While working through your anger and frustration, you start to notice that you frequently snap at people, point fingers at others or stay in your office most of the time instead of interacting with your colleagues. You create a "you" against "them" attitude in your head. You realize that these are all your defense mechanisms to protect your conditioned self who is programmed to seek recognition and appreciation.

You quickly realize that you can't work effectively if you keep yourself withdrawn from everyone or stay sensitive to every comment made in emails, meetings, or conversations. If you do, this place will make your life hell. You also know that you can't force your colleagues to recognize your diligent work and your invaluable contribution to the company.

How can you expand your boundaries, override your conditioned self and face your underlying fears?

Your vulnerability comes from the fact that you think and

believe that you will be disregarded or rejected as nobody recognizes your worth. In order to overcome your fears, take a different course of action that will expose your vulnerability. For example, since your conditioned self is an ambitious person who is looking for recognition, can you scale down your expectations for being appreciated and accepted? Can you be a team player and work together with others, instead of running projects and imposing your ideas on your colleagues to prove yourself? Can you admit to yourself that you went a little too far to get recognized?

When you take some alternative actions that are different than what your conditioned self is used to take, you will get a good sense of your vulnerability. Next step is to build your solid foundation. When you go to work the following morning, can you ground yourself through the bottoms of your feet when the first trigger event, say a criticism from a colleague, pokes at your vulnerability? Can you observe how your thought patterns and belief systems made you feel disregarded or rejected?

Before you respond to your colleague, can you turn your attention briefly to your breath and center yourself, while observing your intense emotions of anger and frustration arise. Instead of immediately launching your defense mechanisms to ward off your colleague's criticism, can you hold off your response a little longer till you calm your emotions?

When you start to feel centered, can you consciously adjust your actions? For example, instead of taking their comment personally and attacking them back with an aggressive reply, can you ask them for clarification? Would you like to know what they really meant by their criticism? Maybe they have a legitimate point and wanted to bring that to your attention.

During this interaction, you will be nervous. You have never asked for clarification before. You always knew how to blame them and defend your conditioned self. You don't know what will happen now. You may feel uneasy and uncomfortable. It's time to re-center yourself. Observe your breath. It's probably short and shallow. Keep observing. Bring your attention inward. Notice how your intense emotions start to overwhelm you again. While staying with your emotions, listen to their clarification. Does it make sense? Would you like to ask more questions? Are they really questioning how good you are, doubting your worth or completely rejecting your opinions?

Keep observing the actions that you take against your defense mechanisms. Make small adjustments and corrections along the way. In other possible trigger events, before you blame everyone for their lack of enthusiasm, can you try to see their point of view? Maybe, some of them don't like their job as much as you do, or, maybe, their conditioned self is not as ambitious as yours. On other occasions, when scaling down your efforts to be recognized and appreciated, try to get less attached to your ideas. You may choose to volunteer less on other projects and focus more on the projects in your department. Keep taking conscious actions with small adjustments and corrections, until you feel that you have a solid foundation where you feel grounded, centered and balanced.

Key Energy: Groundedness

Groundedness is the energy you sense within your mind and body when you feel a rock solid foundation underneath your feet. By just thinking about the bottoms of your feet, you will immediately connect with the earth's energy and feel grounded. Once the connection is established, the strength of the earth's energy will carry you through your practice of grounding, centering and balancing. While connected with the energy of groundedness, the key is to observe your thoughts and beliefs, discover your perceptions that make you believe your conditioned self is under attack, stay with your intense emotions, witness the situation from a distance and then, finally, delay the launch of your defense mechanisms so that you have enough time to adjust your actions.

As you get more experienced in this practice, whatever happens, and whenever you experience challenging situations or face difficult people, you will always be able to connect with the energy of groundedness, create a distance between you and trigger events, and choose your actions consciously.

When you connect with the energy of groundedness, you will feel a sense of separation from your experiences and will be able to witness the actions of your conditioned self and observe the vulnerability of your initial persona. This improved mindfulness comes from having a solid foundation. In order to strengthen your foundation and practice self-observation with a greater efficiency, you need to be able to detach yourself from what is going on around you. Neutralizing your energy creates this detachment.

Key Practice: Neutralizing Your Energy

Neutralizing your energy is like becoming a tree. If you closely observe the mighty trees, you will immediately notice how solid their foundation is. Notice how their roots are strongly grounded into the earth and provide support even during times of forceful storms. Observe how centered they are. Their branches and even trunks bend with gusty winds and then return to their center and maintain their position to hold their ground. In a way, building a solid foundation is to learn how to become a tree. Through the following breathing practice, you will sense that exact neutral energy of groundedness—and will be able to hold your ground when facing trigger events.

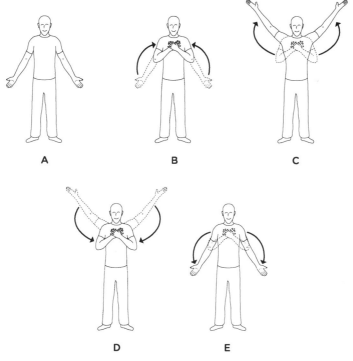

Illustration 14. Becoming a Tree

You can practice this breathing technique either sitting or standing. In the beginning, try to practice this technique standing so that with hand movements you can synchronize your energy flow with your breath more easily. After a while, you will be able to use this technique and neutralize your energy simply by following your breath, and no longer need the hand movements. Then, you can practice this any time, anywhere, whenever you feel the need to neutralize your energy and separate yourself from a situation to witness your conditioned self.

While practicing this breathing technique, just imagine your body having roots growing from your feet into the earth, like a tree. Then, imagine yourself having tree branches growing off your shoulders and head, reaching up to the sky. Now, while inhaling, imagine bringing the earth energy with your breath from the ground into your heart. While exhaling, imagine sending energy with your breath from your heart through your branches to the sky, connecting your heart energy with the sky energies. Then, inhale from the sky into your heart, bringing sky energies into your heart, and exhale from your heart into your roots, connecting again with the earth. This is one breathing cycle.

Any time you would like to neutralize yourself and sense the energy of groundedness, repeat this breathing cycle for three times. At the end of your practice, while staying with this new neutral energy within your body, focus on the bottoms of your feet and feel the earth underneath your feet. Stay connected with the earth for a minute or two. Sense the difference in your energy, in your mind and in your body.

7 · Connecting With Your Inner Power

DURING THE Building Your Solid Foundation phase, you may have experienced that taking actions against your conditioned self and breaking your limiting life patterns is not easy. Even though you may have taken a few conscious actions to override your defense mechanisms, your life patterns may not have disappeared from your life completely. You may still occasionally feel intense emotional discomfort and pain from a trigger event. From time to time, you may still feel that you need to protect your conditioned self's image to hide your vulnerability and disguise your initial persona.

Breaking a life pattern requires many attempts. Until you see a profound and permanent shift in your life flow you have to persistently keep taking conscious steps to expand your boundaries and build your solid foundation. You are almost there though. Most of the work you have done so far will make the rest of the journey much easier and more joyful. You have been climbing this mountain consistently. Be patient since you have a little bit more to go until you reach the summit and have a full view of the meaning of your life and a whole new perspective.

The perseverance and diligence that you need to climb the rest of the way to the summit will come from your inner power.

Even though it may still be difficult to do so, continue making conscious efforts to take actions against your conditioned self and adjust your actions to balance your energy. Imagine a child learning to walk. Have you ever seen a child give up after their first fall? Try to feel what goes through their minds when they fall during their attempts to walk. Do they doubt themselves after every failed attempt? Do they stop trying to walk? NO! Even fall after fall, they do NOT quit. They keep trying, until they eventually stand up and start walking, tall and proud.

Like a child learning to walk, you need to be persistent and resilient. One conscious step against your conditioned self is not going to be strong enough to break a limiting pattern of a lifetime. Your work you have done so far should support you in your attempts to override the programming of your conditioned self at this point. If not, go back and try to expand your boundaries and re-build your solid foundation. But, if you feel courageous and grounded enough to take further actions to unmask your conditioned self, then you are ready to take your next step towards your highest potential: connecting with your inner power.

Connecting with your inner power comes through acceptance—acceptance of your vulnerability. Your inner power will help you stand on your solid foundation with expanded boundaries, and courageously face your underlying fears to minimize their impact on your life.

Process of Acceptance

Acceptance means taking responsibility for who you are. The process of acceptance is *not* about allowing yourself to launch your defense mechanisms and then forgiving yourself for the actions you took. Acceptance involves understanding the defense mechanisms of your conditioned self and embracing your efforts to override your conditioned self for what they are—without any judgment.

Now that you are familiar with the act of balancing through adjusting your actions, apply these principles of balancing to your life more often. When another trigger event hits you—which, you know, it will—be prepared to ground and center yourself and observe what actions you are taking. Is your re-action another one of your conditioned defense mechanisms? Or is it something that involves *doing the opposite*? Observe your actions, understand why you take them and keep adjusting them. Maybe you want to try to go with a less aggressive defense mechanism or you may want to say a gentler *no*. Acknowledge the intensity of your actions and understand how it is related to the level of vulnerability you feel. Simply accept these actions, as they are; not as failures, not as a victim, but with responsibility as a powerful individual.

Through detached self-observation and constant adjustments to your actions, you will be able to face, and eventually, overcome your underlying fears. You now know that your vulnerability is a natural by-product of your life conditioning. You formed your mask to protect your initial persona. So just accept your vulnerability as part of your life conditioning and your conditioned self as part of your coping strategy to hide your vulnerability.

Can you observe your underlying fears and be okay with them? Be certain that anybody who had been in your shoes and experienced the same life situations would most probably have exposed to the same life conditioning, felt the same vulnerability and created a very similar initial persona. It's not your fault that you have them. Don't feel guilty about creating your conditioned self to hide your vulnerability. You have reacted to life according to how vulnerable you felt in each situation you have experienced.

Practicing Acceptance at Home

Suppose that you feel your partner is very controlling. They want to have everything in perfect order at home. You may also care about order at home, but not as much as they do. Whenever you do something that interrupts the order, your partner tells you right away what you did wrong and what you need to do going forward. Every time they correct your actions or words, you get angry. You start to get really frustrated with their tight control over your life.

Whenever you face the trigger event, which may be one of their controlling remarks, you immediately launch your typical defense mechanisms. Every time your partner comments on something you did wrong, you respond with anger and tell them to back off. You blame them for not giving you enough space and flexibility in the house. You don't feel free. Alternatively, you withdraw and contemplate how long you will be able to stay in this *prison*. After launching your various defense mechanisms, you experience conflict and confusion as you start to think about the future and worry that you will never feel free in this relationship. You don't know what to do. You feel you are trapped in this relationship. You feel stuck and confused.

This moment of confusion is the perfect time—and the *opportunity*—to step back from this situation and apply the tools that you have learned so far.

Your intense emotional reactions are anger and frustration. The trigger event is your partner's controlling comments. The thought patterns and belief systems that feed your perceptions tell you that the way you are is not acceptable. You *think* and *believe* that whatever you do is wrong.

When you review your past experiences, you will realize that other situations and people have also made you feel this way. Especially growing up, when your parents constantly pried into your life, you never felt free, independent and successful. They had the best intentions to guide you through life, but you felt that whatever you did was not right, and had to be corrected.

In order to hide your vulnerability and protect your initial persona who is afraid of being judged for doing things wrong, you developed your conditioned self as an independent and carefree person so that you could do things the way you wanted, when you wanted without caring about what others thought. As a result, you, as your conditioned self, did not enjoy doing things in a strict fashion or following others' suggestions—as a reaction to your parents' overly intrusive behavior. Now every time your controlling partner corrects you, you feel like you are back in your childhood—not free, not independent and not accepted as who you are—and your conditioned self feels attacked. Of course, you will want to protect your conditioned self and immediately launch your defense mechanisms and blame your partner.

Now that you have identified your conditioned self and your

initial persona, do you recognize your underlying fears in this scenario? You may have already realized that there may be more than one possible underlying fear that is part of your initial persona. You may fear that you are *a failure*. You think and believe that you can't do anything right. You have developed an independent conditioned self to avoid responsibility for your actions, but deep down, you may fear that you will *not be loved and accepted* if you don't do things correctly or in an order way. Even though your conditioned self doesn't seem to care about what others think of you and your actions, deep down, you may fear that everybody looks at you and judges what you do and how you behave.

These fears, thoughts and beliefs are very intimate. They are all buried within your energy blockages. You have not expressed these thoughts and emotions to your parents or to others close to you. You haven't discussed these thoughts or vented your emotions with your parents nor understood their intentions when you were having these underlying fears growing up. You always felt—and feared—that you were judged and treated like a failure and therefore, not loved and not accepted.

Over time, these repressed thoughts and emotions have become energy blockages, which have attracted very similar situations that poked at your exact vulnerability. Previously, instead of using these situations as an opportunity to decipher your life conditioning, you have blamed your parents, others and most recently your partner. After analyzing the components of your limiting life pattern, you now know why you become so defensive when someone makes you feel like a failure or judges you by correcting your actions or controlling your behavior. You immediately become your initial persona. Feeling vulnerable, you have no choice but to launch your defense mechanisms to protect your conditioned self and hide your vulnerability.

When you realize that you are stuck within this limiting life pattern, next time your partner corrects you, what can you do differently? How can you expand your boundaries? During your next trigger event, can you choose an opposite action where you *thank* them for pointing out what you did wrong, instead of getting angry with them? Such action may be too extreme, but can you genuinely see your partner trying to point you in the right direction by correcting you. If you aren't sure about your partner's intentions, can you simply ask your partner what they mean? Maybe they want to put things in order because they are worried about something. You don't need to agree with their arguments, but can you hear them out and try to understand what he is saying and where he is coming from? You know they are also acting under the programming of their own conditioned self.

Another possible opposite action could be to tell them that what you did is the way you like it. You may gently raise your hand and say that you prefer things around the house to be done in another way. You may start communicating more openly. You may choose to clarify your preference. After expanding your boundaries with some of these actions, when the next trigger event hits you, you may want to ground and center yourself, so that you can calm your emotions and adjust your actions accordingly.

When you start to build your solid foundation, you will notice that you can easily observe your vulnerability when your partner triggers your intense emotional reaction. You can now clearly see the thought patterns and belief systems that feed your perceptions that make you feel attacked.

Since you have more time to observe and recognize the correlation between what your partner does and what your parents did to you in your childhood, can you now stand back and accept your vulnerability? Can you now embrace your defense mechanisms as your tools to protect your free and independent conditioned self? Can you now face your underlying fears and discuss them with your partner? You are getting ready to embrace your past, accept your life as it is today and move forward towards your highest potential.

The following technique will help you deepen the process of acceptance and face your underlying fears at a deeper level.

What If? So What?

You can accept your vulnerability and own your underlying fears through four magic words: "What if? So what?"

The purpose of this *what if* question is to face your vulnerability and test how much you are able to face your underlying fear. It's a very simple technique: whenever you feel vulnerable, think about the worst-case scenario and ask yourself, *what if* the worst-case scenario occurs? Answer your question with *so what*. What could possibly happen? Then, observe your emotions. Do you notice your underlying fears magnified when observing the worst-case scenario? Do you feel comfortable with responding to the worst-case possibility with *so what?* If not, why not? What is it really that you are afraid of?

Continuing from the above example, you can apply *What if? So what?* as follows—note how each question tests a course of action and challenges a possible worst-case scenario.

- *What if my partner controls my actions all the time? So what?*

- *What if I will never feel free again? So what?*

- *What if someone makes me feel like a failure when I do certain things? So what?*

- *What if everyone judges my actions? So what?*

- *What if I told my partner that I prefer doing things this way? So what?*

- *What if I told them that I feel like I'm judged all the time? So what?*

- *What if I thanked them for pointing out what I could do better? So what?*

- *What if I told them that I fear that I'm a failure and they will not accept me? So what?*

- *What if I confessed that I take my partner's corrections as a lack of love? So what?*

When you ask yourself so what, your underlying fears will be magnified and another possible worst-case scenario will appear in your mind. How can you handle that worst-case scenario? Can you accept your vulnerability and face your underlying fears?

You now know that your conditioned self gets defensive and exaggerates the situations and people's reactions because of your underlying fears. While going through this exercise, notice that the worst-case scenarios are not as bad as your mind makes you believe. The possibility of some of the worst-case scenarios happening is very low, but, they look and sound very real to you. They make you feel even more vulnerable. Can you say, "Yes, I'm afraid of being a failure, being not good enough, not accepted, and not loved?" Understanding that these are just thought patterns and belief systems of your initial persona and are not reality, can you connect with your inner power and accept your vulnerability?

The technique *what if—so what* is very effective in getting into the depths of your underlying fears. When you face those intimate thoughts and beliefs that are part of your initial persona, it is okay to feel overwhelmed. Don't feel inferior that you have certain fears. This process is the natural progression of peeling off the layers of your life conditioning. Everyone goes through this process. Everybody is in the same boat. There are no exceptions. Don't compare yourself to others as some people can hide their vulnerability very well. After all, everybody hides behind the mask of their conditioned self. Just focus on your work. You will connect with your inner power when you start accepting your vulnerability.

Accepting instead of Positive Thinking

Facing your underlying fears may be difficult. Due to this difficulty, at times, you may prefer replacing your fears with positive statements. Instead of facing your underlying fear of, say, continuing from the above example, being judged and treated like a failure, you tell yourself that you are a successful, independent person whom everybody accepts and respects. Actually, this strategy is a short-term patch and not effective in the long run. The system of life will soon bring you another trigger event. While facing the challenging situation or the difficult person, your positive statement will not sustain the high energy level necessary to stay grounded. Without grounding and centering, you will not be able connect with your inner power.

In order to permanently raise your energy level, you need to stay with your intense emotions and face your underlying fears to overcome your vulnerability. Instead of denying your underlying fears, or your vulnerability for that matter, observe them and accept them as they are. Forcing yourself to think positively about yourself or others who have triggered your vulnerability will separate you from the trigger event, cover your underlying fears further and ignore the mask of your conditioned self. This forceful action will keep you from accepting your vulnerability. As a result, you will not be able to connect with your inner power.

When you depend on positive thinking to cover your underlying fears, you may end up using your positive thoughts as another defense mechanism. You can only raise your energy level permanently, when you gain a greater understanding of your life conditioning and gain deeper insights into your underlying fears. By staying with your underlying fears, you can say, "I emotionally react this way, because I have this particular vulnerability." In that moment, you simply accept the reality that your intense emotional reactions come from your underlying fears and are part of the effort to defend your conditioned self.

When you accept your thought patterns and belief systems, your intense emotional reactions and your defense mechanisms as they are, you start accepting your conditioned self as someone you have created to disguise your initial persona. When you recognize your initial persona and accept its vulnerability, the need for the mask that protects it becomes unnecessary. When you realize that you don't need the mask anymore, you stop defending your conditioned self. The energy you preserve by not defending will raise your vibration and connect you with your inner power even more. You are getting ready to allow your authentic self to naturally emerge. But before you can start fully expressing your authentic self, you need to learn how to communicate assertively.

Assertive Communication

Assertive communication is a direct form of interaction that focuses on expressing facts. It is the willingness to share exactly how you feel and what you think—without needing to criticize or try to change others' opinions or force them to think or feel a certain way. Unlike your other defense mechanisms that repress your true thoughts and emotions, the assertive communication is to express them fully and powerfully.

You initially may find assertive communication absolutely horrifying and impossible to do. Don't worry! Everybody, on their journey, goes through this difficult phase. In order to liberate yourself from the reins of your life conditioning, you need to powerfully communicate your true thoughts and emotions to others. If you don't feel comfortable in the beginning, don't force yourself to tell everything you think and feel to the outside world. First, connect with them internally. Write them in your journal. Say them out loud when nobody is around. Stay connected with them. Accept them as they are.

Next time, when you have an opportunity to assertively communicate your true thoughts and emotions, just try to focus on what you think and how you feel and say it. That's all. No one will—or should—blame you for thinking and feeling a certain way. You now know that whenever there is a resistance to practice a technique, you need to turn your attention inward. If you can't practice assertive communication, ask yourself what you are afraid of? Why do you feel vulnerable? What are your initial thought patterns and belief systems that prevent you from communicating assertively? Maybe there is another underlying fear of your initial persona that you haven't identified before. Always remember, any resistance, any blockage is a great opportunity to get to know yourself and eliminate the energy blockages that are holding you back.

Over time, you will notice that communicating assertively gets easier to do. You just need to express your thoughts and emotions as they arise within you, without a filter, without a mask. Instead of getting angry or complaining or making a long face, will you be able to say, "When you look at your cell phone in the middle of our conversation, I feel neglected and not loved" or "When you repeatedly ask me to organize my desk, I feel controlled and powerless."

When you face your vulnerability and accept it as a natural occurrence resulting from your past life experiences, you will realize that having your thought patterns and belief systems, and therefore, your underlying fears is so *normal*. You don't need to hide your true thoughts and emotions anymore. Connect with your inner power and tell others how their actions or words make you feel.

A true assertive communication is only possible when you have a solid foundation and are connected with your inner power. When you are grounded and centered, you can detach yourself from your opinions and from the need to be right. Then, you can easily adjust your actions and shift your focus onto the purpose of the interaction with others, instead of exerting your energy to protect your conditioned self. Then, you can use your excess energy to enjoy each other's company, learn from each other, come up with solutions to problems, bring resolutions to conflicts, collaborate on new ideas—possibilities are endless. When you are communicating assertively, you respond to discussions with an open mind using facts. You bring to the table an honest representation of your true thoughts and emotions without any hidden agenda. You express yourself with power and integrity, but without the need for control of others or promotion of your conditioned self.

Key Energy: Inner Calmness

Being emotionally vulnerable is the biggest roadblock that stands in the way of discovering your authentic self and living a joyful and fulfilling life—your highest potential. By accepting the vulnerability of your initial persona and recognizing your conditioned self as someone you have created to disguise your initial persona, you are able to connect with your inner power. You can now overcome your underlying fears.

By going through the process of acceptance and integrating assertive communication into your daily routine, you start to feel safe enough to handle any trigger event that may come your way. This feeling is powerful. With it, you can change the course of your actions, consciously. You feel that you are ready to face your underlying fears without yielding to them. When you are connected with your inner power, you can stay grounded and centered and choose your actions consciously and communicate your true thoughts and emotions assertively without a fear.

Right at the time when you feel this deep connection to your inner power, observe the beautiful inner calmness that spreads within your energy body as you take actions to break your limiting life patterns. That inner calmness comes from knowing that no trigger event can make you feel vulnerable again. That inner calmness sets in from realizing that you are powerful enough that you don't need to defend your conditioned self and disguise your initial persona anymore. Energetically feel this deep inner calmness in every cell in your body. That energy is your inner power.

Key Practice: Inner Power Meditation

Now let's experience that inner calmness through a meditation practice. The following technique will connect you with your inner power and let you feel the inner calmness in every cell in your body. During this meditation, you will direct your energy throughout your body. Therefore, your focus needs to be sharp to direct the energy flow to the part of your body that you work on.

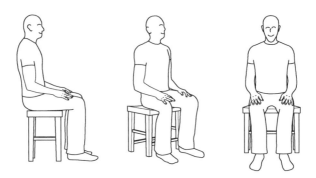

Illustration 15. Inner Power Meditation

You can practice this inner power meditation instead of the energetic expansion meditation in the mornings. After you finish your self-observation meditation practice, you will only need to change your hand positions, placing your palms on your thighs, facing down. Maintain the same posture, your back, neck and head are straight in one line. Similar to energetic expansion meditation, start allocating about five minutes to inner power meditation every morning, following your self-observation meditation practice.

In case you prefer to practice this meditation separately, first find a comfortable place to sit. Then, place your feet flat on the floor at shoulder width apart. Your knees are at a ninety-degree angle. Your back is in upright position, straight but not stiff. Your shoulders, neck and head are all relaxed.

Place your hands on your thighs, palms facing down. With your palms resting on your thighs, keep your arms relaxed. Elbows can be bent to keep your arms fairly relaxed and free of tension. Now, take a deep breath in, and when exhaling close your eyes. Now, place your tongue gently on the roof of your mouth and put the tip of your tongue behind your front teeth. Keep your mouth closed, breathing naturally.

Observe your thoughts and images as they pass through your mind. Acknowledge them. Try to stay detached and indifferent to your thoughts. Now, start to relax your body. Slowly go into a deeper relaxation by releasing the muscle tension from your feet, calves, knees and legs. Again, by directing your attention and energy, relax your upper body, first your belly, then your stomach and chest. Next, relax your arms and shoulders. As you release the tension from your shoulders, let the deep relaxation spread into your neck and head.

Now, visualize a ball of light (or an energy ball) hovering a few inches above your head. Examine its color and brightness. Keep your focus on that ball for a while and imagine its energy expanding. Slowly direct this ball of light to descend through the top of your head into your head and face. Sense a strong energy flowing and opening every cell on your head and face to higher vibrations. Note that wherever your attention goes, energy flows there.

Imagine this ball of light expanding within your body. Let it flow into your neck and shoulders, then, into your arms, all the way down to your fingertips. Then, direct this ball of light to flow within your upper body—your chest, stomach and lower belly. Now, let it flow into your legs and all the way down to the bottom of your feet and to your toes.

Next, focus on the bottoms of your feet. Stay focused for a few seconds. Feel the solid foundation you have built underneath your feet. Do you feel the strength the energy of the earth is providing? Do you feel the safety and comfort that comes from standing on this solid foundation? Do you feel grounded? Do you feel centered?

Now, it's time to bring this strong energy to the core of your body. Slowly let your energy flow up, from the bottoms of your feet to your ankles, then through your knees and thighs to your lower belly and your stomach. Visualize this powerful energy flow activating your life force energy center and solar plexus in the core of your upper body.

Once these energy centers are activated, you will sense an inner calmness radiating from the core of your body to every cell in your body. Acknowledge this inner calmness. Stay connected with the sensation of inner calmness spreading through your body. Along with the inner calmness, some of the more common sensations include tingling, a cold or warm breeze or a subtle moving sensation within the body. If the sensations become uncomfortable, you can redirect your focus to the bottoms of your feet and connect with the earth to ground yourself—and stop your practice.

While the sense of inner calmness is spreading through your body, notice the deep relaxation you feel in every cell. Now, in this deep calmness, acknowledge the process of acceptance that you have gone through. Gently visualize where in your life you can further accept your vulnerability and the things as they are.

Recognize how your vulnerability affects your life. What kind of worst-case scenarios are you are dealing with in your mind? Can you challenge those worst-case scenarios with "so what?"

Go through your life situation and see where you can assertively communicate your true thoughts and emotions. What could happen? What is the resistance? What are you afraid of?

To finish your meditation practice, place your hands on top

of each other and put them on your life force energy center. Imagine that you are bringing the expanded energy back to its source and putting a lid on top to preserve it. Take three deep breaths in, then exhale slowly and gently.

Connect with the earth's energy through the bottoms of your feet. Feeling grounded and connected to the earth, feel the inner calmness within your body once more. Feeling connected with your inner power, open your eyes, and stretch for a minute or two to let your physical body experience this new energy.

8 · Expressing Your Authentic Self

NOW THAT YOU HAVE BUILT a solid foundation and connected with your inner power, it is time to start taking concrete steps toward expressing your authentic self. In a sense, you have talked the talk, and now let's walk the walk.

When you're asked to express your authentic self, some of you may panic for a moment and think, "Oh no, I don't know who my authentic self is yet. How do I express what I don't know?" Don't worry, you don't need to know exactly who your authentic self is. The emergence of your authentic self will be a natural progression of your journey. Step-by-step, you will feel the qualities of your authentic self unfold in your life.

During the previous phase, you were able to connect with your inner power and assertively communicate your true thoughts and emotions to others. That deep connection with your inner power will help you feel your uniqueness within you and prepare you to incorporate your true essence into your life. At this point, you are now ready to liberate your authentic self and strengthen your steps towards your highest potential. Your next step is to start living joyfully.

Living with Joy

You may still be wondering what exactly you need to express and how you can realize your authenticity. There is no concrete answer to your question other than to just express *your uniqueness*. The concept of uniqueness is powerful. No one can tell you who you are or what your authenticity is. You have to explore it yourself. It is your authenticity. The good thing about your authenticity is that you don't need to acquire it from somewhere or learn it from someone. It is within you.

In order to reach in and grab onto your authenticity, all you need to do is to watch for the opportunities that life presents to you. As a result of the work you have done so far, your energy level is very high at this stage of your journey. At this high frequency, life will generously offer you numerous opportunities where you will get a chance to connect with your authenticity. You may already be experiencing these interesting opportunities showing up in your life. Some of these opportunities will provide circumstances where you discover your interest in art, engage in a new hobby, attend an exciting workshop, connect with your passion and inspirations or have a chance to display your creativity. Seize the moment and grab onto the opportunity to be your authentic self, as these circumstances are most likely aligned with your essence. It's time to start living with joy.

On the other hand, you may have not noticed any opportunities that seem to be aligned with your essence. Or there may be some opportunities in front of you, but you don't feel a strong connection to them. You may be puzzled over which opportunity to choose. What do you do in these situations? How do you ensure that you choose the right opportunity? How do you bring more opportunities that are aligned with your authenticity into your life? By understanding your values. Your values will guide you to bring joy into your life and allow you to be your authentic self.

Recognizing Your Values

You live according to your values. A value is a concept, thought, belief, mission or point of view on life that you hold to be important and meaningful. The set of values you have motivates you and directs your actions. Whether you realize it or not, whether you are happy or not, your choices in life are based on a particular set of personal values. The way you honor your values and the priority you give to each of them may change from time to time. The important point here is to recognize what type of values you are honoring at any given time and how your actions reflect these values in your current personal and professional life.

While contracting your boundaries and hiding your vulnerability, you have adopted a set of values based on your life conditioning at the time. Even though, some of these values are not aligned with your authentic self, they have helped you protect your initial persona and reinforce the mask of your conditioned self.

Let's say that, per your life conditioning, one of your underlying fears is being dismissed. Therefore, you have adopted "recognition" as one of your core values. In order to honor that value, you work hard, you study diligently, you earn degrees, and you compete intensely, so that you get enough recognition and acceptance to disguise your initial persona.

Suppose that when you were little, you observed how

successful your dad was at his job, so you thought you needed to also have "security" in your value set. In order to honor this value, you chose your subject of study according to how secure a future it would offer or you chose your profession because it promised financial success. When you look at your life today, you may realize that all of these values—recognition, security and predictability—are at play. You may be in a profession, such as accounting or finance, where your conditioned self can comfortably honor these values.

Recognizing the values that you're currently honoring in your life will tell you how you got where you are today. The real challenge is to start honoring the values that are more aligned with your essence. Part of your unhappiness and discomfort in your current situation comes from the fact that there is a dissonance between what values you currently honor and what you'd really like to honor. You need to find authentic values that represent your essence.

In order to help you with this value clarification process, let's separate values into two distinct sets: mind values and heart values. While reading each category, observe what values you honor and what values you feel are missing right now in your life. This review of your values will help you tremendously in figuring out what direction to take and what opportunities to embrace that are more aligned with your authenticity and bring joy into your life.

Let's go over the mind values first.

Mind Values

Mind values come directly from your life conditioning. They are aligned with your survival instinct to protect your conditioned self. You adopt this set of values to address your underlying fears. Most of the time, they are geared towards satisfying the needs or wants of others, or towards complying with social expectations and pressures.

You can recognize these values through the frequent use of the word "should" or "must" or "have to" when they come up in your life. Your mind values are not necessarily all bad, though many are restrictive to your authentic self. Their purpose is to keep you within the identity of your conditioned self and make you stay under the influence of your life conditioning. You just need to identify and understand how they have affected your current life situation.

Heart Values

Heart values come from your essence. These values are free of life conditioning. They are aligned with your authentic self. They represent your essence. They don't carry fear. Ask yourself "What would I love to do if I knew there was no chance of failing, being judged, rejected, or dismissed?" The answer will definitely spring from a heart value.

You can recognize heart values because they are typically expressed by the use of the word "want" or "would love to". Growing up, you have suppressed these values as you have put the needs and expectations of others above your own and conformed with their rules. You have made your decisions based on others' wishes or hopes. You have adopted your mind values as the guiding principles of your life and given up your heart values. As you have drifted away from your essence, you have forgotten what your own dreams, inspirations, desires, needs, goals and aspirations are.

Adopting New Values

Your authentic self will only emerge if you start taking actions to honor those values that are important and meaningful to your essence. When you don't identify and clarify your values, a conflict arises between your mind and your heart. Your mind will say, "You should always keep this job. Look, it pays the bills." On the other hand, your heart will say, "But, I'm unhappy here, I don't want to do this job, I rather be working in nature, or helping others, or doing charity work, or organizing book clubs." What can you do?

Your goal is to strive for a healthy balance between your mind and heart values. Depending on where you are in your journey, some of your mind values will still be applicable to your current life situation, and you feel that you need to keep honoring them to continue with the trajectory of your life flow. That's okay. Just acknowledge where you are. You may want to continue to work at your day job, because your dominant mind value is predictability and recognition, while you start to allocate more time, whenever you get a chance, to creativity, which is one of your heart values. You may even find new areas within your current job that you can use your creativity or other heart values that you'd like to honor. Keep exploring ways to bring your heart values to life.

In another possible scenario, let's say you are an artist. Contrary to the above example, you have creativity as one of your mind values. You feel that, through your creativity, you *should* be famous and financially independent one day. When you pressure yourself to be creative to honor your mind values, you may find yourself frustrated, confused and conflicted. Instead, you could choose to accept your creativity as one of your heart values and connect with joy and purpose while performing your art. You can celebrate your creativity and give yourself a chance to be famous one day—not as a goal, but as a by-product of your creativity.

Be careful about not pushing or forcing yourself into a particular activity just to connect with a heart value. Instead, first observe what you're drawn to. Note that this connection is always mutual. You feel drawn to and the opportunity draws you in. Just observe what kind of opportunities you have in front of you. What *feels* more joyful and fulfilling? When having a conflict between your different values, just look at your heart. What is it that you'd like to do? What *feels* like the right opportunity?

The distinction is often very subtle. Let's say that one of your heart values is to help others. Instead of trying to enroll in a certification program to become a counselor or a therapist, connect with the feeling of *doing* it. Understand what attracts you about counseling as a career. Investigate how you will feel doing it day in, day out.

At this high energy level, once you decide to honor a heart value, certain opportunities will appear in front of you. Be alert and when a particular book, course, or mentor shows up in your life, take advantage of it. Step through the door and embrace the opportunity. Treat every opportunity as an experience. Keep your focus on honoring your creativity or any other heart value you want to connect with. You don't have to quit your job, but at least you can align your mind and heart values, so that you can find more balance in your life.

Connecting with your heart values will definitely increase your energy level even more and bring a sense of joy into your life. The higher your energy level, the more heart values will emerge. Recognize, honor and incorporate those new heart values that are aligned with your essence into your life. Over time, you will see that your mind values seem to lose their importance.

The purpose of realizing your authenticity is to live your life according to the principles of your essence so that you can find joy and fulfillment in your life. You can only get to experience the meaning of your life through the expression of your authentic self. This phase is pivotal because it may very well introduce you to your life's work. As you start expressing your essence, you will slowly come to realize the unique thoughts, visions, talent, creativity and skill set that you naturally and innately possess. You just need to take actions to apply them more consciously to your life.

This kind of deep connection with your essence is rejuvenating. It injects a very powerful energy into your actions. When you are filled with enthusiasm and have a new outlook on life, you want to get up in the morning and start your day as soon as you can. This rejuvenation pushes you into an exhilarating creative process. You may find yourself connecting with old inspirations and dreams that you once had. New visions, ideas and aspirations will push you further into new areas of interest. You may start nurturing your old interests and incorporate them into your life. Follow your creativity. This is the birth of your authentic self and your life's work. Claim your uniqueness and keep walking towards your highest potential, joyfully.

Expressing Gratitude

Once you start living joyfully and using every opportunity to honor values aligned with your essence, you will start to observe your life from a different angle. Through this new perspective on life, pay attention to what is already working for you, instead of dwelling on what is not. Instead of focusing on what you don't have, acknowledge what you have. Connect with the energy of gratitude to appreciate the things that flow in your life. Be grateful for the new skill sets you are discovering as part of your authentic self. Be grateful for your creativity that is blossoming. Be grateful for the glimpses of joy and fulfillment that you may have started to feel at work or in your relationships.

Gratitude is such a powerful energy. You connect to that energy by not just appreciating what you have and who you are today, but also by getting in touch with the meaning of your current life and by appreciating your life as the accumulation of every person you have met and every situation that you have experienced over the course of your lifetime.

Through your journey so far, you have gained the deep understanding and inner knowing that life reflects exactly what your energy level is. Without the study of your life experiences, without having lived your past and without becoming aware of your conditioned self and initial persona, you wouldn't be able to access such deep understanding and inner knowing—your wisdom. You owe gratitude to your past experiences, as without them you would not be able to create this knowledge base to launch your transformation journey and have a chance to fully express your authentic self. Acknowledge your past life experiences as preparation for your authentic self. Be grateful for every moment of your life.

While taking actions to break your limiting life patterns, notice and acknowledge the subtle shifts that you are creating in the flow of your life. Observe these shifts with increasing gratitude as you start to experience firsthand how you can improve the flow of your life by overriding the actions of your conditioned self and raising your energy level. Notice how life is supporting your transformation journey by responding to the increase in your energy level with a better flow. Acknowledge that. Own your part of the equation by taking more powerful and conscious steps toward expressing your authentic self. Then simply allow the system of life to bring you the opportunities that facilitate the change.

Be grateful for this understanding and realization of how much control you have over your life. Be grateful for life, for its support along your journey, and for the self-realization you are going through. As you break your limiting life patterns and make changes, notice how life brings you these subtle shifts to support your intentions for a positive change in your life. Be grateful for this new insight and experience that life is in perfect order, in beautiful balance, and in magnificent design.

Believe in the power you have—the change you desire is in your hands.

Spreading Love and Compassion

When you start living with joy and feel gratitude for the life you have had and the life you are having, love and compassion for others come naturally from your heart. This deeper connection with others is another powerful sign that you have started expressing your authentic self. You have waited until this phase of your journey to show love and compassion to others because it is very difficult to do so without feeling love and compassion *for yourself* first. As your authentic self naturally emerges and you understand your own life conditioning, love and compassion will flow naturally from within you to the world around you.

With greater self-knowledge and deeper understanding of your life conditioning, you are ready to acknowledge others' paths. You can recognize their emotional pain and suffering. You notice how they are stuck in their limiting life patterns. You now understand why they show their intense emotional reactions. You see how they repeat the same, self-sabotaging behaviors as part of their own journey.

When you start spreading love and compassion, you notice three particular actions that come from your heart. These are: *being in their shoes, listening attentively* and *accepting others with respect*. All of these actions are well aligned with your authentic self. Review them and see if you can easily implement them in your life. However, it's okay, if it is difficult to do so. It just means that you still feel vulnerable. If that's the case, simply observe your actions, thoughts, beliefs and emotions of your conditioned self. Whenever it is difficult to show love and compassion, notice your vulnerability and recognize the underlying fears that feed the actions of your conditioned self. In those moments, gently try to find ways to bring more of your authentic self into situations you are dealing with.

Being in their Shoes

Understanding others is a necessary component of spreading love and compassion. Any relationship is a great opportunity to practice the principles of understanding and empathy. When you look at some of the arguments that you and your partner constantly have in your relationship, you will easily notice that everybody, including you, is stuck within their own point of view—to protect their conditioned self. Now that you have completely understood the mask your conditioned self is wearing, can you stay grounded and centered and understand where others are coming from?

Like the self-observation practice that you have applied during your self-awareness process, can you witness others from a distance? Without judging them, can you discover their perceptions that are also fed by their initial thought patterns and belief systems? From your experience in your journey so far, you know that blaming others for triggering your intense emotions is a defense mechanism. Probably, their defense mechanisms work exactly the same way. They, too, want to hide their vulnerability and disguise their initial persona. Do you notice it?

If you have established your connection with your inner power, you will be able to stay grounded and centered, as well as detached, whenever you find yourself in conflicts. While witnessing such situations from a distance, can you try to see a different angle that others may be coming from? Observe how a particular situation personally affects others. Try to put yourself in their shoes and connect with new insights into how they have arrived at their opinions. By understanding each other's point of view, everyone has the ability to work together to come up with effective resolutions to any conflict.

Listening Attentively

In attentive listening, you stay present in the conversation by paying attention to almost every word the other person is saying. You stay with the conversation. While listening you don't bring any of your interpretations, your perceptions, your labels, your judgments, your life conditioning into the interaction. That way, you can stay neutral, interested and curious—but detached.

You may feel that attentive listening requires a big effort and a lot of attention. Like the time when you started practicing the self-observation meditation, in the beginning, you will need to spend some time to quiet your mind and observe your thoughts while trying to stay in the conversation. Over time, you will notice that attentive listening is a key component of how you interact with others. When you stay in conversations with an alert mind and focused attention, you will feel that your energy doesn't get drained as much. As a result, you feel a deeper connection to the person with whom you are interacting.

Every communication has two directions. One direction is where you express yourself to the other person, and the other direction is where you receive what the other person is trying to express. When you master assertive communication by expressing your true thoughts and emotions as they come from your heart and also master attentive listening at the same time, you will soon notice the change in the energy in your relationships. Love and compassion is now becoming a tangible component of your life.

Accepting Others with Respect

When you gain a deeper understanding of others and their situations, you will begin to drop all labels, judgments and perceptions you have for them. This shift in your perspective happens not only in your relationships, but also in all other aspects of your life. When you get rid of the conditioned lens, through which you have been looking at life, acceptance naturally follows. You have less of a tendency to take things personally. You will be less likely to be threatened by disagreements with others. You accept everything and everybody as part of the flow of life. You reach this beautiful state of mind, where you start to see people as they are and respect their ideas as simply another valid or possible point of view, even though they may be totally different from yours.

Accepting others with respect is easier said than done. If you truly feel your inner power, you will not be offended by anybody's point of view, attitude or any other differences that you perceive. Since you no longer feel the need to protect your conditioned self, you will be able to gain a deeper insight about others and accept them exactly as they are, appreciating where they are on their journey, where they are coming from in terms of their emotions, thought patterns and belief systems, what their needs are and what values they are trying to honor. You will love connecting with such deep insights. Try it!

You are now ready to open the door to your authentic self and introduce your uniqueness to the world.

Key Energy: Interconnectedness

With understanding and acceptance of who you are and the meaning of your life, you may have already started to feel a deeper connection with everyone around you. From your own observations throughout your journey, you may have begun to realize that we are all the same in many ways. We deal with the same life issues, struggles, vulnerability, underlying fears and defense mechanisms. There are no exceptions. We all feel emotional pain and suffering.

Never stop observing your thoughts and emotions. Recognize whenever you show an intense emotional reaction towards anyone. Notice whenever any glimpse of judgment appears in your mind when interacting with someone. Acknowledge whenever you label someone for what they think or who they are. Be in their shoes. Listen to them attentively. Accept them with respect. Compassionately connect with their path and understand their life conditioning. You know, deep in your heart, that we all want to feel safe, we all want to feel connected, and we all want to feel loved.

No matter what happens, try to apply the Golden Rule—treat others the way you want to be treated. The Golden Rule sets a very high standard for your actions. Be aware that you tend to cross the line of the Golden Rule when you feel vulnerable and a perceived attack of a trigger event activates your underlying fears. Acting out of fear, you disregard the Golden Rule. Therefore, don't feel guilty or ashamed if you can't apply the Golden Rule in every action you take, but notice your vulnerability every time you violate it. Keep working on and use these moments of confusion as your opportunity to get to know your conditioned self and embrace your vulnerability that caused you cross the line. To get out of the confusion, connect with your inner power and allow your authentic self to re-emerge with joy, gratitude, love and compassion. Feel how connected you are with life. Feel how interconnected we are with each other.

Key Practice: Heart Meditation

The following meditation will connect you with your heart energy center and help you energetically connect with joy, gratitude and compassion. By keeping your focus on the center of your chest where your heart energy is you will be able to raise your energy to connect with your essence. After practicing this heart meditation, you will sense a deeper connection with joy of life, gratitude for the things you have, and love and compassion for others as you feel deeper connection in your relationships.

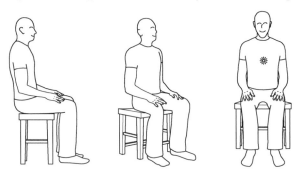

Illustration 16. Heart Meditation

You can practice this heart meditation after you finish your self-observation meditation practice at night, before you go to sleep. You will only need to change your hand positions, placing your palms on your thighs, facing down. Maintain the same posture, your back, neck and head are straight in one line. In the beginning, allocate about five minutes to heart meditation every night, following your self-observation meditation practice.

In case you prefer to practice this meditation separately, first find a comfortable place to sit. Then, place your feet flat on the floor at shoulder width apart. Your knees are at a ninety-degree angle. Your back is in upright position, straight but not stiff. Your shoulders, neck and head are all relaxed.

Place your hands on your thighs, palms facing down. With your palms resting on your thighs, keep your arms relaxed. Elbows can be bent to keep your arms fairly relaxed and free of tension. Now, take a deep breath in, and when exhaling close your eyes. Now, place your tongue gently on the roof of your mouth and put the tip of your tongue behind your front teeth. Keep your mouth closed, breathing naturally.

Observe your thoughts and images as they pass through your mind. Acknowledge them. Try to stay detached and indifferent to your thoughts. Slowly place your concentration on the center of your chest. Try to keep your focus on that point throughout your entire practice. If you are distracted by your thoughts and lose your concentration, bring your attention back to the center of your chest, re-focusing on your heart energy center.

After keeping your focus on the center of your chest for a while, you may feel a subtle flow within your body. The undivided attention will activate the energy within your heart energy center and enhance the flow of energy of joy, gratitude and compassion within your body. What you may feel varies from person to person. Some of the more common sensations include tingling, a cold or warm breeze or draft, subtle moving sensation within the body. If the sensations get too intense, you can redirect your focus to the bottoms of your feet and connect with the earth to ground yourself and stop your practice.

When your energy level increases and your energy expands out of your heart energy center. You will sense ripples of energy waves spreading from your chest out to each corner of your body. Just acknowledge what's going on. Observe and witness the sensations, but still keep your focus on the center of your chest.

Now, at this expanded energy level, connect with your heart values. Imagine yourself honoring these heart values. Visualize how they can bring more joy into your life. Notice the opportunities in front of you that you can easily embrace to express your authentic self. Do you feel a particular opportunity that pulls you more strongly than others? What kind of heart values would you like to honor in your life? What would be the fun and joyful thing to do that will give you a chance to express your authentic self?

After connecting with joy, mentally review the current flow of your life. Observe how your deeper understanding of your life conditioning makes your life so much more meaningful. Notice how your thought patterns and belief system are no longer affecting your reactions as much. Bring more gratitude into your heart for the new skill sets that you have been discovering lately. Be grateful for the journey you have undertaken. Can you feel a deeper connection with your life, with your work and in your relationships? Are you more grateful for some of the people in your life? Do you recognize any part of your life that is working well?

Let the energy keep expanding and moving out from your heart energy center embracing everything and everybody around you. You may see some faces or situations that need your compassionate attention. Extend your love and compassion to them.

Keep sending love and compassion from your heart energy center, to each individual, one by one, with whom you would like to resolve a particular conflict. Can you understand where they are coming from? Can you feel their vulnerability? Let the energy of love and compassion you are sending embrace their vulnerability. Can you recognize their conditioned self in action? Through your heart, show them the way to joy, gratitude, love and compassion.

To finish your meditation practice, place your hands on top of each other and put them on your life force energy center. Imagine that you are bringing the expanded energy back to its source and putting a lid on top to preserve it. Take three deep breaths in, then exhale slowly and gently.

Now, connect with the earth through the bottoms of your feet. Feeling grounded and connected to the earth, feel joy, gratitude, love and compassion in your heart once more. Now, slowly open your eyes, and stretch your body for a minute or two to let your physical body feel this new energy.

9 · **Stepping Into New Beginnings**

YOU HAVE finally met your authentic self. Now, you know how to utilize the opportunities life offers to bring aspects of your uniqueness into your life. Throughout your journey, you have experienced that the higher your energy level is, the better the life flow is. All you need to do is to take actions that raise your energy level and bring joy and fulfillment into your life. Life will take care of the rest and guide you to your highest potential.

Imagine a musician trying to get perfect pitch by adjusting their instrument—tightening and loosening the strings until they feel satisfied by the sound. Your journey toward being your authentic self is much like this tuning process. When you reach your perfect pitch, meaning that you maintain the connection to your essence for longer periods of time, you will be able to express your unique authentic self as it naturally manifests in every aspect of your life. In a sense, these manifestations are the beginning of a major life transformation.

In order to keep your connection to the higher energy levels, you must consistently work on expressing your authentic self. New beginnings represent the ever-increasing moments of that joyful and fulfilling expression of your authentic self. It's not simply one door that you need to go through to step into a new beginning. It's a gradual path that you proceed along throughout your journey in different aspects of your life. *It's not merely a total change of life, but a change in the way you see life, how you respond to life, how you experience life.* Step into new beginnings. Expressing your authentic self is new. Connecting with your heart is new. Following your essence is new. Finding your unique and authentic place in the world is new.

Acknowledging Synchronicities

When you start becoming your authentic self, the frequency of the synchronicities you experience in your life will increase. Synchronicity is simply a moment when you feel a sense of alignment between seemingly unrelated things. You feel very connected when you experience a synchronicity. Just joyfully observe these random things coming together and opening doors for a magical flow. Acknowledge them. They are fun and joyful; some examples might include:

- *finding convenient parking spots in the busiest time of the day*

- *running into an old friend who introduces you to someone who teaches the kind of martial art you wanted to practice*

- *finding a book on the table at a coffee shop that you intended to buy a long time ago*

- *randomly finding out about the course you always wanted to take starting the following week*

- *somehow finding tickets to a sold-out lecture of someone whom you have been following for years*

Illustration 17. Roller Coaster vs River Ride

Before you started your journey, life was like a rollercoaster. With frequent ups and downs, moments of happiness followed moments of despair. One day you felt everything made sense, and the next, you found yourself confused. Sometimes you felt that your partner was the best thing that ever happened to you, and other times you questioned your relationship. After traveling on this journey for a while, you are starting to sense that the flow of your life is turning into a comfortable river ride. Frequent and abrupt ups and downs have been disappearing from your life lately. Through the synchronicities and the opportunities that are aligned with your essence, a smoother flow is appearing in your life.

Focusing on the Experience

At times, though very rare now, you may lose this smooth ride and bring that roller coaster ride back to your life. The reason for this fall back to old times is that you may be confused to see many opportunities in front of you. When you become your authentic self and move forward at this high energy level, many opportunities will show up in your life. You may not know which opportunity to choose or what door to go through. When you overanalyze the situation you may fall into despair. In these moments, just follow your intuition. Over time, you will intuitively sense more and more what opportunities are aligned with your essence.

Your focus should be on the experience. Just choose one opportunity at a time that feels most aligned with your authentic self. Forget about your goal of why you chose that opportunity. Focus on the experience the opportunity offers. Soon, you will see another set of doors appear in front of you. Try to sense each door's alignment with your essence. Try to envision the experience that each door will provide. Which opportunity exerts a stronger pull on you? Which one feels more joyful? Which one feels right to your heart?

If you realize that you have chosen a door that is not leading you down the path you thought it would, then, learn from your experience, close that door, and open another one. No problem. At the end of the day, every opportunity is a life experience that will expand your self-awareness and deepen your wisdom, even though you don't recognize its lessons or benefits at the time.

Remember, you are an energy being. As long as you take steps, you will attract new opportunities. Opportunities will never cease to appear in your life unless you hold yourself back from taking actions. You now know that when you feel vulnerable and are afraid of getting out of your comfort zone to expand your boundaries, that's the time you need to take a deeper look at your conditioned self and your initial persona. Understand how your underlying fears influence your mood, your actions and the direction you are going. Do you recognize your insecurities, worries, self-doubt, or anxiety when you are afraid of taking actions?

The art of walking through doors is to focus on the experience, not the result, and use this experience as another way of getting to know your conditioned self, understanding your life conditioning and the vulnerability of your initial persona, and also as an opportunity to express your authentic self. Therefore, the pressure of having to choose the "right" door is unnecessary. At the end of the day, since your focus is on your experience, there is no right or wrong door. Each door is just an opportunity to experience your self; either your conditioned self or your authentic self or a bit of both.

Life Long Process

When you truly embrace each opportunity as a chance to express your authentic self, your energy level naturally rises. At that level, you start to connect with your life's work or become more productive at your current job. You start to deepen your connection with your partner in your relationship or find your soulmate. You choose to get involved with a non-profit organization or work on community projects. You decide to take on new hobbies or explore your creativity in different artistic expressions.

You begin to study new subjects that nurture your essence. You follow a healthier lifestyle, be more joyful and active in your life. You start to appreciate life as it is and be grateful for what you already have. You feel a sense of fulfillment and inner calmness that stems from knowing who you really are.

These beautiful experiences and magical moments of synchronicities are only a glimpse of what lies ahead for you. Enjoy these experiences that your current energy level attracts to your life. At the same time, remember that the journey towards your highest potential is a life-long process. Never abandon your self-observation practice, never stop meditating, never quit taking conscious actions to face your underlying fears and break your limiting life patterns.

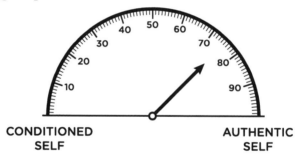

CONDITIONED   AUTHENTIC
SELF   SELF

Illustration 18. Authenticity Meter

From time to time, you may still notice that your conditioned self reappears in your life. Observe your actions. Mentally look at the authenticity meter. Where do you stand? How authentic or conditioned are your actions? You may experience that, as your authentic self, you have gone three steps forward and caught a glimpse of your highest potential. Then, some time later, you notice that you have retracted one or two steps back. This back and forth is very normal. It's due to the change in your energy level as you switch between your conditioned self and authentic self.

Any time you feel you have contracted your boundaries again and fallen down to a lower energy level, use this withdrawal as an opportunity to recognize the mask of your conditioned self and the vulnerability of your initial persona. Through grounding and centering, reconnect with your inner power adjust your actions and bring your authentic self back to your life. Observe your actions and constantly ask yourself who is in charge now, your conditioned self or your authentic self?

Life is all about getting to know your Self—your conditioned self and initial persona—and to fully embrace life is all about being your authentic self.

Key Energy: Trust

You are probably feeling it already. When you step into new beginnings, you are filled with joy and hope. It feels like you are starting your life just now. You have the enthusiasm and motivation of someone, who is about to graduate from high school or college with hopes, aspirations and dreams. Notice some of the grand possibilities that have already started showing up in your life. Experience the glimpses of the magical and harmonious flow in your life.

All of a sudden, life starts to bring opportunities that seem like miraculous coincidences. Explore whatever resonates with your heart. Instead of trying to *become* this, or that, *honor* your heart values that make you feel complete. Notice and acknowledge the real connection that exists between your energy level and the quality of your life experiences. Well immersed in your journey by now, you realize the wisdom deep within you that, when you get to know your Self and understand your life conditioning, you can release your energy blockages, raise your energy level and break your limiting life patterns.

The knowledge and the realization that there is a system that aligns your energy level with your life experiences without any failure will deepen the trust in yourself that you are in charge. The wisdom you have acquired through your journey will ultimately foster your trust in life. Trust eliminates fear and empowers you to release all of your attachments and expectations. You feel like you can surrender to the system of life because you know it will take you to your highest potential. Through this trust and surrender you sense a deep fulfillment and inner calmness. Every part of life is you, and you are every part of life.

Key Practice: Authentic Self Meditation

The following meditation will deeply connect you with your authentic self and its manifestation in your life's work. It requires constant concentration on your third eye, which is the point between your eyebrows at the top of your nose. This point is the energy center for intuitive intelligence—your innate wisdom. By keeping your focus on your third eye, you will feel a subtle expansion of energy in your body that will connect you with the energy of your authentic self and glimpses of your new beginnings. After practicing the authentic self meditation, you will sense a deeper trust in life and in yourself.

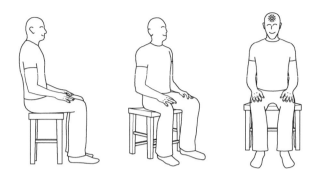

Illustration 19. Authentic Self Meditation

You can practice this meditation after you finish your self-observation meditation practice in the morning, alternating with your inner power meditation. In the beginning, you can allocate five minutes to it. After you finish your self-observation meditation practice, you will only need to change your hand positions, placing your palms on your thighs, facing down. Maintain the same posture, your back, neck and head are straight in one line.

In case you prefer to practice this meditation separately, first find a comfortable place to sit. Then, place your feet flat on the floor at shoulder width apart. Your knees are at a ninety-degree angle. Your back is in upright position, straight but not stiff. Your shoulders, neck and head are all relaxed.

Place your hands on your thighs, palms facing down. With your palms resting on your thighs, keep your arms relaxed. Elbows can be bent to keep your arms fairly relaxed and free of tension. Now, take a deep breath in, and when exhaling close your eyes. Now, place your tongue gently on the roof of your mouth and put the tip of your tongue behind your front teeth.

Keep your mouth closed, breathing naturally.

Next, start gradually relaxing your body. Relax your feet, your ankles, your knees, your legs, your upper body, your stomach, your chest, then your shoulders and arms, and finally your neck, head and face. As you feel the relaxation in every muscle in your body, start observing the thoughts and images that are going through your mind. Stay detached and indifferent to your thoughts. Now, gently bring your focus onto your third eye.

After keeping your focus on your third eye for a while, you will feel a subtle energy expansion within your body. The undivided attention will activate your life force energy, raise your energy level and enhance the flow of energy within your body. What you may feel varies from person to person. Some of the more common sensations include tingling, a cold or warm breeze or draft, or a subtle moving sensation with the body. If the sensations get too intense, you can redirect your focus to the bottoms of your feet and connect with the earth to ground yourself.

Whenever you get distracted or pulled away by your thoughts, ask yourself what you are thinking right then. Notice and acknowledge what your thoughts are. This question will create a break between you and your thoughts. Within that brief moment, you will be able to take a step back from your thoughts and bring your attention to the bottoms of your feet to ground yourself for a few seconds. Once you feel grounded, you can refocus on your third eye.

A little while later, you will feel energy expanding from your third eye. Invite images of your authentic self into your mind. Either observe the glimpses of your authentic self you start to acknowledge in your life or visualize how your future looks like with your authentic self evolving and taking more opportunities to express itself. Through the intuitive intelligence that you have activated in your third eye, connect with the images of your new life flow, of your new beginnings. Where do you see your authentic self is going from here? How can you allow your authentic self emerge even more?

While you are visualizing these images, observe the sensations of deep calmness and trust embrace your body. While still keeping your focus on your third eye, connect with the images of your authentic self being engaged in your life's work. What kind of life's work do you see intuitively that you are doing? Don't force anything. Simply imagine how it will feel like to follow some of the opportunities that are in front of you right now. Anticipate where each one of these opportunities may lead. Feel the connection with your essence. Do you feel, energetically, how being your authentic self brings joy and fulfillment to your life?

Observe how your authentic self could take more steps towards your life's work. What kind of steps do you visualize taking? What kind of opportunities would you like to receive? What kind of customers or clients would you like to have in your business venture or workshop? What kind of engagements, assignments, or community work would you like to get involved? What kind of creative outlet would you like to use for the new skill set you may have discovered? What kind of location do you visualize to have your business or practice to operate from? What kind of new doors would you like to see in front of you? What kind of activities and projects do you see yourself getting involved? Keep connecting with your third eye to see some of these visions of your authentic self and your life's work.

Now observe your emotions. Are you excited or worried? Are

you enthusiastic or hesitant? Are you motivated or withdrawn? Slowly, bring more visions of your authentic self to your mind and observe your emotions at a deeper level. Recognize through your intuitive intelligence that life is the reflection of your energy level. What kind of actions feels right to you to raise your energy level? Connect with trust in the wisdom you acquired in your journey. Trust that life supports you to be your authentic self. Trust that your authentic self can do the things you visualize. Trust in your connection with a better life flow. Trust in life. Slowly let the energy of trust dispel your concerns, worries and anxieties. Now simply surrender. Surrender to life. Imagine yourself, opening your arms and welcoming life as it is and allowing yourself to be your authentic self.

To finish your meditation practice, place your hands on top of each other and put them on your life force energy center. Imagine that you are bringing the expanded energy back to its source and putting a lid on top to preserve it. Take three deep breaths in, then exhale slowly and gently.

Now, connect with the earth through the bottoms of your feet. Feeling grounded and connected to the earth, feel the energy of trust and wisdom that you have felt during your practice. Now, slowly open your eyes, and stretch your body for a minute or two to let your physical body feel this new energy.

You can practice authentic self meditation whenever you would like to attract new opportunities, new doors, new projects, new directions, and new energies into your life. The key is to fully trust in the system of life and completely surrender to it. No attachment. No expectation. Just sit in your meditation and imagine that you are opening your arms for what life has to offer to you in your new beginnings.

So Long Seeker!

Writing this manual is just another aspect of my life journey that I could never have predicted. In many ways, the challenge of writing about the system of life has taken me through the journey all over again. Now, again here I am, overjoyed and humbled as I recognize where life has guided me.

Through the study of your own life experiences, I hope you have also realized that whatever you experience today is exactly what your energy level has pulled into your life. You now know that it is not a coincidence. The situations are only here so that you become aware of your conditioned self and initial persona, understand your life conditioning, recognize your underlying fears and accept your vulnerability and finally become your authentic self to start living with joy and fulfillment.

You and I have walked side by side throughout your journey. I hope you have fully connected with the key energies of each phase. It's okay, if you haven't. Just go back to that specific phase you didn't quite connect with, and review the material until you feel and sense that special energy. Brick by brick, step by step, you can constantly advance your journey to higher energy levels. You know by now that the journey is not linear. It's a life-long process. No matter where you are in your journey, always remember that roadblocks are only there for you to learn more about your conditioned self and initial persona and give your authentic self a chance to emerge stronger. Never forget that you can always connect with your inner power to bring more joy and fulfillment into your life. Just keep walking on this beautiful journey.

Through your diligent study of each phase, you have been detecting and releasing your energy blockages, one by one. Yes, in the beginning it felt counter-intuitive to think that pulling such challenges and dramatic events into your life was for your own good. But now, having released your energy blockages, raised your energy level, and slowly transformed from your conditioned self into your authentic self, today, you fully experience the positive shift in your life flow. You are now beginning to understand the meaning of your life.

From here on out, the only action you need to take is to open your arms and heart to receive the opportunities your higher energy level has started attracting into your life. Then, simply walk through each door that is aligned with your heart to express your authentic self. Joyfully share your essence and uniqueness with the world and people around you.

Going forward, fulfillment and inner calmness will be your companions as you live your authenticity. Radiating joy, gratitude, love and compassion from your heart, you now know that everything is indeed in harmonious flow and within perfect order. Everything and everyone is interconnected. All in all, life embodies all aspects of you as you embrace all aspects of life.

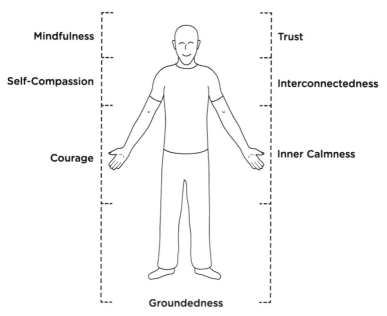

Mindfulness

Self-Compassion

Courage

Trust

Interconnectedness

Inner Calmness

Groundedness

Illustration 20. Key Energies around the Body

Books That Inspired Me

The Power of Now (1997) by Eckhart Tolle

Spiritual Growth (1989) by Sanaya Roman

Biology of Belief (2005) by Bruce Lipton

Memories, Dreams, Reflections (1989) by C. G. Jung

Same Soul, Many Bodies (2004) by Brian L. Weiss

You Can Heal Your Life (2002) by Louise L. Hay

PNI—The New Mind/Body Healing Program (1993) by Elliott S. Dacher

Power vs. Force (2002) by David R. Hawkins

No Boundary (2001) by Ken Wilber